Pure-Hearted

The Blessings of
Living Out God's Glory

Marah —
I hope my book
blesses you —
Kathy

Endorsements

Sometimes as we work enthusiastically in the vineyard, we can get stuck in our own expectations and 'noise.' Kathy Collard Miller's new book *Pure-Hearted: The Blessings of Living Out God's Glory* is a beautiful, faith-filled source of insight, stories, and Scripture helping us unclutter our inner motivations and feelings so that we can focus on blessings, which put us in a better position with God's divine purpose. In each gracefully written chapter, she leads us deeper into a place of greater purity. And through each discussion question and real-life example, she helps us put aside expectations that stem from our oh-so-human inclinations to focus with more clarity on God's glory and grace.
—**Maureen Pratt**, Author of *Peace in the Storm: Meditations on Chronic Pain & Illness*.

Full of wonderful wisdom, practical application, and spiritual insights. A must-read for both the new Christian and the seasoned believer. I highly recommend this book for individual or group study.
—**Linda Wood Rondeau**, author of the futuristic thriller, *The Fifteenth Article*.

Kathy Collard Miller writes in a comfortable manner, as if she sat with her reader over a cup of coffee at the kitchen table. The quiet profoundness of her thoughts are well written, Biblically based ones we can each embrace.
—**Julie B Cosgrove**, Award-winning Christian author, speaker, and devotional writer.

In Kathy Collard Miller's book, *Pure-Hearted: The Blessings of Living Out God's Glory*, she challenges readers to inventory the heart with the goal of more closely reflecting God's nature in our daily life. She does this while assuring us of his unwavering love and commitment to us. It's a fascinating—and successful—combination. When we are certain of our place in his kingdom, we are free to be transparent with ourselves and others. Self-examination is often painful and discouraging, as the realities of our walk with Christ fall pitifully short of his example. Kathy makes this a joyful journey as she weaves the Father's love with the call of Christlikeness. Tired of playing a role? *Pure-Hearted* will help you move into the authenticity that is Jesus.
—**Deb DeArmond**, writer and speaker, *Related by Chance, Family by Choice, I Choose You Today: 31 Choices to Make Love Last,* and *Don't Go to Bed Angry. Stay Up and Fight!*

How can I live out God's glory? It all starts with a pure heart. Not an easy task, considering how tainted my motives can be even when I have good intentions. Author Kathy Collard Miller identifies nine blessings that start with a transformed heart and end with God getting BIG glory. I can't wait to gather a book club to discuss Kathy's book, *Pure-Hearted: The Blessings of Living Out God's Glory*.
—**Kathy Carlton Willis**, author, speaker, and God's Grin Gal.

I was immediately engaged reading the true stories and then personally challenged by the questions and reflections calling me to engage in self-evaluation, not just read the book. Chapter 5 spoke to my guilt-ridden temptation to be a perfectionist. I loved this statement by the author, "Don't let perfectionism diminish or destroy growth in being satisfied with God's good gifts." What a powerful truth. Here you will find answers and simple application challenges that will facilitate healthy life changes for greater joy, peace, and contentment with yourself, others, and most importantly, in your relationship with Jesus Christ.

—**Doreen Hanna**, Founder and President, Modern Day Princess.

Most Christian women desire a holy heart, but we lack the "how to." *Pure-Hearted: The Blessings of Living Out God's Glory* reveals God's truth and the paths required to find freedom from day-to-day challenges and temptations that cause fear and despair. Kathy Collard Miller offers biblical insight, virtuous hope, and wise words to help us walk the walk while we talk the talk. A must read for those who desire to become a "woman after God's own heart."

—**Laura Petherbridge**, Speaker and author of *When 'I Do' Becomes 'I Don't', The Smart Stepmom, 101 Tips for The Smart Stepmom*, and *Quiet Moments for the Stepmom's Soul.*

Our actions or reactions can be hurtful to us and those we love. Kathy does an excellent job helping us to realize that by giving glory to God, during our most painful situations, he will give us healing peace. It is at that time we can fully love others as God loves us! Truly a healing book!

—**Lee Ann Mancini**, Author and adjunct professor, South Florida Bible College and Theological Seminary, Deerfield Beach, Florida

With warmth and humility, Kathy Collard Miller shares stories about herself (and others) that will both warm your heart and encourage you to draw closer to the Lord. You will also find biblical examples in each chapter, as well as discussion and reflection questions, making this a perfect study for individuals or groups. Reading this manuscript has blessed and challenged me, as I know it will do for you.

—**Kathi Macias**, Award-winning author of more than fifty books, including *40 Day Devotional Challenge.*

As godly women, we long to glorify God, but if we are honest, we know we often fall short—sometimes very short. Kathy comes along beside us and says, "I've been there, and I've learned a few things that have helped give me a pure and renewed heart as I journey toward a God-honoring life." *Pure-Hearted: The Blessings of Living Out God's Glory* is a gift to those who desire to know our great God in greater truth and to see ourselves as He sees us.

—**Cheri Cowell**, Author of *Parables and Word Pictures in the Following God series, 365 Devotions for Peace,* and *One Story, One Mission, One God Bible study*

Kathy Collard Miller's book, *Pure-Hearted: The Blessings of Living Out God's Glory*, is a thought-provoking read. She guides us to know our inner selves better and to come to the root of something that is bothering us even if we don't realize what is causing our frustration. The questions at the end of the chapters help us to look deeper into what we have read and be able to use the material to not only benefit ourselves but those around us.

—**Jann W. Martin**, Commissioned Associate in Ministry from Trinity Lutheran Seminary, Award-winning Christian children's author, speaker, and teacher.

Your spirit yearns to give glory to God, never ceasing. Kathy's book, *Pure-Hearted: The Blessings of Living Out God's Glory*, is an excellent guide on how to give God glory. But what does glory look like? How do we give our God glory? Do we acknowledge God as the source of any good we do? These are just a few of the questions Kathy seeks to answer. The key, as she so beautifully explains, is to surrender again to God's plan to help us be pure-hearted. Though we will fail, God wants to equip us to represent him thus making a difference in our lives-which ends up bringing him glory! I highly recommend anyone who wants to have a pure heart before God to read this book.

—**Lane P. Jordan**, Best-selling author/international speaker/Bible teacher/Life Coach

"Purify my heart" are words most Christians sing with sincerity. In her latest book, Kathy Collard Miller lovingly explores our mixed-up heart motives often hidden even from ourselves. If you want to glorify God and grow more like Jesus, I recommend you read this thoughtful book, respond to God's Spirit, and rejoice in serving him from a pure heart—it is possible and it is what God desires.

—**Poppy Smith**, Inspirational Speaker, Award-winning Author, Christian Life Coach, *Go For It: Make Your Life Count for God.*

Kathy Collard Miller takes readers on a journey to conduct their own spiritual heart surgery—identifying potential cancers, removing toxins and allowing healing in such a way that gives glory to God during the process.

—**Michelle Lazurek**, Author of *An Invitation to the Table.*

I liken Kathy's insights to that of Jeremiah's call of God to His people. *Like a farmer breaking up hard unplowed ground ... just as a farmer must clear away thorns lest the seed is wasted, you must get rid of the sin that is ruining your lives* (Jeremiah 4:30 NET Bible). Like Jeremiah, Kathy, in her transparency, can lovingly reach deep, clear away debris, and get to the heart of many familiar issues in our lives; those hidden secret places of the heart we do not yet perceive. In so doing, the revelations bring freedom to love him more, love ourselves and others better. Kathy helps us see how to seek and give God greater glory through his cleansing and sanctification process. Such a refreshing read!

—**Merry S. Streeter**, author and illustrator of *Lolly's Fish Tale; When She Meets a Bully Face to Face.*

Kathy Collard Miller brilliantly unpacks the difficult and elusive concept of God's glory. She plummets the reader into the depth of their raw motives to allow the loving Father to reveal truth and bring glory to himself. *Pure-Hearted: The Blessings of Living Out God's Glory* is a well-balanced weaving of Kathy's own stories, excerpts from well-known authors, and substantiated with her selection of scripture. These have created the perfect mix for the reader to grasp that we are a reflection of God's glory. Kathy says: "My desire in this book is for us to inspire others to know our great God in greater truth." Kathy, I say, "You have hit the mark."

—**Heidi McLaughlin**, International Speaker and author of five books including *Restless for More: Fulfillment in Unexpected Places.*

Kathy's book inspires readers to know God in greater truth and to see God glorified as he works in our lives, purifying our motives. Based on Scriptures, this book gives an in-depth study with nine "s" words—including self-controlled, satisfied, and ending with surprise. All the "s" words lead us to examine how to gain God's power for daily living. *Pure-Hearted: The Blessings of Living Out God's Glory* is a go-to-guide to develop pure motives for right living and glorifying God.

—**Peggy Cunningham**, missionary and author of *Dancing Like Bees.*

Pure-Hearted

The Blessings of
Living Out God's Glory

Kathy Collard Miller

Elk Lake
PUBLISHING, INC.
PLYMOUTH, MASSACHUSETTS

Cover Design: Jeff Gifford
Interior Design: Cheryl L. Childers
Editors: Susan K. Stewart, Deb Haggerty
Published in Association with Suzy Q Inc.

PUBLISHED BY: Elk Lake Publishing, Inc., 35 Dogwood Dr., Plymouth, MA 02360

Library Cataloging Data
Names: Miller, Kathy Collard (Kathy Collard Miller)
Pure-Hearted: The Blessings of Living Out God's Glory, Kathy Collard Miller
234 p. 23cm × 15cm (9in × 6 in.)
Description: *Pure-Hearted: The Blessings of Living Out God's Glory,* challenges readers to inventory the heart with the goal of more closely reflecting God's nature in our daily life while assuring us of God's unwavering love and commitment to us.
Identifiers: ISBN-13: 978-1-946638-29-8 (e-bk.) | 978-1-946638-42-7 (POD) | 978-1-946638-43-4 (Trade)
Key Words: motives, purity, character, God's glory, change, commitment, God's love, Fruit of the Spirit
LCCN: 2017949817 Nonfiction

Dedication

To my brother, Chuck Collard
December 12, 1952-January 8, 2017

Bro, your passion for the Lord was motivated by your desire
for God's glory. You represented Jesus with joy and trust. I'm so
grateful you were in my life.

Table of Contents

Foreword

I am honored and thrilled Kathy invited me to write the foreword for this powerful book. Let me give you some quick background. Kathy and I have been acquainted for many years, but in recent years we have discovered a remarkable convergence of the message God is building into our lives, and our friendship has grown in light of that shared passion. This book, *Pure-Hearted: The Blessings of Living Out God's Glory*, continues to unpack that message with biblical integrity, wisdom, clarity, and remarkable insight.

Let me ask you some questions about your heart's journey. Do you find yourself struggling with the same patterns of behavior year after year? Do you fall short over and over and feel like a failure—hopeless to really change? Perhaps you have even made peace with what you used to try to change. Maybe you now say, "That's just who I am. Nobody's perfect." But, deep down, you know that very pattern has brought chaos into your relationships and discord into your thoughts and emotions. Maybe you have come to feel captive to the emotions, responses, and reactions that seem to have a life of their own beyond your control.

Or, maybe you haven't thought it out in such detail. Maybe you simply know you want more of the power and presence of the living, indwelling Jesus. You long to grow in him, and be more available to him for his great purposes.

If you have picked up this book, I think you very likely are hungering for more of him in the details and moments of life. You want to grow beyond mere knowledge of the Bible into intimacy with the Lord of the Scripture. In the truths expounded in the pages of this book, you will find the secret to the communion for which your heart was formed.

We have certain phrases we sprinkle liberally throughout our church vocabulary, yet would be hard pressed to really define. I love to take those apart and see what the substance really is. This is something Kathy does brilliantly. Can you define what it means to "give God the glory"? You will be able to after studying this book. What does it really mean to be "pure hearted"? You will know exactly what that means after studying this book. What does it really mean to have "right motives"? How do you allow the Spirit to "search your heart"? Kathy gets to the heart of these profound truths and they will take on new depth for you, and acquire new dimensions.

In *Pure-Hearted*, Kathy Collard Miller invites us to join her in a journey to freedom. That is God's goal for us. Call it purity. Call it glory. Call it what you will, in the end, it is freedom. Freedom from our small vision. Freedom from our petty responses. Freedom from our need to control. Freedom from our need to defend ourselves. Freedom from everything in our human nature that holds us in its grip and diminishes us. Freedom to be all that Jesus paid so high a price for us to possess.

You will find fresh insight into familiar Scripture; practical application of rich truth; a keen understanding of our very frail human nature; and, above all, a penetrating acumen in defining the

Holy Spirit's work to move us from living in the confines of our human nature into the great expanse of his power and presence.

Jennifer Kennedy Dean
Author of the best-selling *Live a Praying Life*®
Executive Director of The Praying Life Foundation

Acknowledgments

I'm so grateful for so many who encouraged me in my journey of writing this book:

Thank you to Gayle D., Karen D., Pam F., Joy H., Merry S., and Barbara J. for reading portions and giving me wise input.

To my fabulous editor, Susan K. Stewart at Practical Inspirations, thank you, for I know Pure-Hearted would not be as clear, concise, and meaningful without your corrections, guidance, and wisdom.

I can never thank enough Deb Haggerty, publisher, Elk Lake Publishing Inc., for supporting my vision and seeing the potential of Pure-Hearted. Deb, you inspire me with your desire for God's glory in your life and publishing ministry. I praise God for the privilege of co-laboring with you and calling you friend.

A supportive agent like Shawn Kuhn is invaluable for guidance. Thank you, Shawn, for being available.

My beloved husband, Larry, is my cheerleader and wise counselor. He gives me thoughtful input that guides my thinking. Honey, even though your name isn't on the cover, our lay counseling ministry together provides the foundation and skeleton of the ideas and insights for this book. I'm so grateful we are "in life and ministry" together.

Including God the Father, Jesus the Savior Son, and the wise counselor, the Holy Spirit, in the Acknowledgments is almost ridiculous—a no-brainer. But truly, I fully know and am convinced whatever this book might accomplish is by God's will and design. Both in the ideas expressed and in any transformation within a reader's heart. Truly, truly, truly, it is all to God's glory.

Introduction

On Christ's glory, I would fix all my thoughts and desires, and the more I see of the glory of Christ, the more the painted beauties of this world will wither in my eyes and I will be more and more crucified to this world. It will become to me like something dead and putrid, impossible for me to enjoy.[1] —John Owen

I was watching my nine-year-old grandson, Raf, create his own version of a computer game and amazed at a third grader's computer skill (which I didn't have), I exclaimed, "Raf, you are amazing!"

Raf immediately replied, "No. Only God is amazing."

I was so amazed, oops, thrilled, to hear his comment because it's the truth. Raf had inadvertently given God the glory he deserves. And Raf's comment reminded me of my own desire to give God glory.

That's why I've written this book. I believe I'm not alone. I believe you are considering or reading this book because you want to bring glory to God, who alone deserves to be called "amazing."

Unfortunately, I think superlative words like awesome and amazing can be overused in general conversation, thus diminishing the power of describing God in ways only he is qualified to claim. In their book *Burning Hearts: Preaching to the Affections*, Josh Moody and Robin Weekes write:

> We live in a time when everything is "great" and "wonderful" and "brilliant." And yet if we use superlatives to describe the mundane, how do we describe the one who is altogether lovely? So, here's something we are trying to do: reserve our superlatives for the Savior. That is to keep the utmost language for our utmost Treasure, and to borrow whatever language we can to praise Him who is[2].

I've been trying to do that after hearing a sermon many years ago encouraging the same idea. I had never thought of it before but now there's a little check in my spirit by the Holy Spirit when I succumb to using a word for the mundane that should only describe God's character.

But that's only a small—yet significant—way all of us can magnify God. I believe the primary way we can give God glory is to purify more and more our heart's motives. Out of the Spirit-purified well of our heart's condition, we will know more freely and wisely how God wants to use us to exalt, lift, and magnify his holy nature. You could say we'll be pouring the pure water of truth into a muddy pool thus clearing it more and more of wrong desires, motives, and actions. That very process will give God glory.

Sometimes, we are unclear about what brings glory to God and how to bring glory to God. In the first chapter, we'll explore how our goodness, walk of faith, and directing attention to God are three of many ways. But there isn't any "one size fits all" way to glorify God. Otherwise, this book would only need one chapter: "The Secret Formula for Glorifying God in One Step." Instead, we must abide moment by moment seeking the Holy Spirit's leading thus glorifying him as our source.

There is also no guarantee God's work in us will be acknowledged by others. Thankfully, God's glory is not dependent upon their reaction or beliefs. We cannot force anyone to agree with us nor give credit to God, even if we were to perfectly reflect a perfect God.

Additionally, we cannot diminish God's glory even when we reflect him imperfectly because of our mistakes, sins, or problems. Regardless, the angels continue to call God Almighty "holy, holy, holy" before his throne. His perfection has not changed. At the end of time, every knee will bow before him, acknowledge him and give him glory.

But what is God's glory? James M. Hamilton Jr. writes, "I would suggest that the glory of God is the weight of the majestic goodness of who God is, and the resulting name, or reputation, that he gains from his revelation of himself as Creator, Sustainer, Judge, and Redeemer, perfect in justice and mercy, loving-kindness and truth."[3]

The stars reveal his splendor. Common grace offers his blessings to all. The gifts and talents he gives to undeserving people exalt him even though the gifts may be misused. Sometimes, I'm brought to tears hearing the beauty of the singing voice or the incredible musical skills of an orchestra. Anyone need only pay attention to the numerous ways God reveals himself as holy and good—then the reason to give him glory is seen.

Ultimately, we only need to see the perfect life of God's redeeming Son Jesus.

When Jesus had spoken these words, he lifted up his eyes to heaven, and said, 'Father, the hour has come; glorify your Son that the Son may glorify you, since you have given him authority over all flesh, to give eternal life to all whom you have given him.

And this is eternal life, that they know you the only true God, and Jesus Christ whom you have sent. I glorified you on earth, having accomplished the work that you gave me to do.' John 17:1-4

Jesus is God himself, and on earth, he was an exact representation of God the Father. Although we will never represent God perfectly like Jesus did, he still wants to use us. What a glorious calling. And in God's generosity, he "shares" his glory by changing us to be more like him.

My desire in this book is for us to inspire others to know our majestic God in greater truth. In each chapter, we'll see how God is glorified as he works in our lives, purifying our motives.

In Chapter 1, we'll begin *seeking* some important ideas about how we can become more aware of our heart's motives.

In Chapter 2, instead of being selfish, we'll recognize how God loves us unconditionally. We will be *selfless* knowing he will be glorified.

In Chapter 3, instead of fighting God's will, we'll acknowledge God's wisdom in designing his plan. We will *surrender* knowing he will be glorified.

In Chapter 4, instead of doubting our importance to God and his kingdom, we'll identify our identity in Christ. We will be *secure* knowing he will be glorified.

In Chapter 5, instead of being disgruntled, we'll know God's goodness. We'll be *satisfied* knowing he will be glorified.

In Chapter 6, instead of being emotionally unsettled, we'll claim God's strength. We'll be *stable* knowing he will be glorified.

In Chapter 7, instead of a lack of discipline, we'll apply his power. We'll be *self-controlled* knowing he will be glorified.

In Chapter 8, instead of forgetting God's qualities, we'll worship him. We'll be *struck* in awe knowing he will be glorified.

In Chapter 9, instead of being undependable, we'll call upon his faithfulness. We'll be *steadfast* knowing he will be glorified.

In Chapter 10, instead of being unaware of God's workings, we'll realize he's using us. We'll be *sensitive* to representing him knowing he will be glorified.

In Chapter 11, I'll share a little *surprise* God showed me that makes for a great wrap up of this book.

Each chapter ends by focusing on a Biblical character or group along with individual/group discussion questions.

In my description of the different chapters above, did you notice something? Each chapter's goal for bringing God glory is an "s" word: selfless, surrendered, secure, satisfied, stable, self-controlled, struck with awe, steadfast, and sensitive. To gain God's power to see those nine "s" words real in our daily living, I'll be encouraging us to evaluate our underlying heart motives. Pure motives welcome the Spirit's power for right living.

I haven't attained the ability to always see those qualities in my life or perfectly giving God glory, but I want to learn more. I'm hoping you'll join me.

—Kathy Collard Miller

Chapter 1
Start the Purification

'Glory to God' was the theme of the angelic hosts that announced Jesus' birth to the shepherds in the field and of the heavenly throng whose songs John recorded in Revelation. What a privilege almost beyond imagination that the all-majestic God calls sinners like us to contemplate his glory and to echo the angels' chorus in our own worship[4].—David VanDrunen

What is the chief end of man? Man's chief end is to glorify God, and to enjoy him forever.—*Westminster Shorter Catechism*

I stood with the other women singing at the women's retreat where I was speaking, sensing God's presence and beauty. As we lifted our voices in a song about desiring God's glory alone, I thought, *Lord, I'll go through anything with joy and love if it will bring you glory.*

And I meant it. Except at the end of the retreat.

Going through the evaluations from the one hundred women, I read comments about the speaker—me—which were encouraging and positive. I continued to scan through them with a smile on my face because God had used me for his glory. Praise the Lord.

Then one comment caused me to stop turning to the next evaluation. I focused in on the writing. "This speaker is crazy. She should never be a speaker."

Crazy? Never be a speaker? Me? Can't be.

Why did she write that? I wanted to scream. *What did I do wrong? How did I offend this woman?* But there was nothing else in her answers giving me a clue.

I set the pile of forms on the table and with a crooked smile, said a final goodbye to the retreat chairwoman. She complimented me again for my ministry with them, but the word "crazy" swatted away her words like a home run batter swinging at an easy curveball.

That crazy word "crazy" haunted me all the way home. I knew her comment shouldn't bother me. Ninety-nine percent of the evaluations had been positive. The chairwoman was pleased. God seemed to be pleased.

I even told myself the truth: "Her evaluation doesn't define me. I am only supposed to concentrate on pleasing God. She doesn't determine whether I obeyed him. Most people love my vulnerable sharing about that 'crazy' time in my life when I was out of control with anger toward my daughter. Most likely, my story offended her. Maybe she was abused herself. That's it. I must have reminded her of her abuser."

My defensive litany went on and on. I felt rejected and dejected. *What happened to my desire to only bring glory to God? Why did I start making it all about me?* My murky motives were revealed. I obviously had a more restricted definition of what would bring God glory. God wanted to bring himself glory through criticism. I didn't.

Over a time of seeking God and his opinion, I could receive God's empowering to see myself and my ministry through God's eyes even while surrendering to however he wanted to purify my heart.

I have a feeling even if you haven't experienced something similar because you're not a speaker, you want to bring glory to God with a pure heart. Yet eventually you stood in a pool of murky and muddy motives.

- Maybe you sang a song about bringing glory to God yet later in the day yelled at your husband for disregarding your opinion.

- Maybe you vowed to never again respond impatiently while driving but then cursed under your breath at the fool of a driver who almost hit you on the freeway.

- Maybe you cheerfully went through a hard time believing God would be glorified. Yet afterwards, someone gossiped about you saying you were a hypocrite because of your previous failures. In turn, you criticized her to another friend.

No, we aren't going to become perfect, but we can trust God to make a difference in our lives—which will bring him glory. His faithfulness will continue to pursue us and change our hearts.

At times, we *will* respond in the Holy Spirit's strength. Even then we may be tempted to make it all about us. After all, when we're focused on the Lord, we notice there are benefits—like the fruit of the Spirit. Then we feel guilty. Did we only want the benefits from wanting his glory?

The Apostle Paul writes at least two times specifically about the results of being motivated to bring God glory. And those results in turn bring God glory.

In his second letter to the Thessalonians, he writes:

To this end we always pray for you, that our God may make you worthy of his calling and may fulfill every resolve for good and every work of faith by his power, so that the name of our Lord Jesus may be glorified in you, and you in him, according to the grace of our God and the Lord Jesus Christ. (2 Thessalonians 1:11-12)

Paul uses the word "resolve" (ESV) to indicate a desire (NIV, NASB) for "good and every work of faith" (vs. 11) in order to have God glorified (vs. 12). "Resolve" in the Greek can also be translated as "prompts" (NLT), and other words indicating motive. In other words, the more we desire God's glory, the more we'll take hold of the Holy Spirit's inner impulse to cooperate with him, knowing it will glorify God and bless us. In that verse, we might think "good" (vs. 11) only refers to others but goodness and works of faith benefit us also.

Secondly, Paul writes to the Philippians:

And it is my prayer that your love may abound more and more, with knowledge and all discernment, so that you may approve what is excellent, and so be pure and blameless for the day of Christ, filled with the fruit of righteousness that comes through Jesus Christ, to the glory and praise of God. (Philippians 1:9-11)

Commentator Matthew Henry writes about Paul's words, "The things which most honour God will most benefit us." In God's power we'll love others more, have greater knowledge and discernment, and identify what is best (excellent).

Is God's Glory All that Important?

Yes, it is. The word "glory" is mentioned ninety-one times in the New Testament epistles alone, which doesn't even include the numerous variations like "glorious." The New Testament letter writers obviously thought the concept of God's glory was important. We discover the different ways we experience God's glory and then reflect his majesty to others, like a microscope and a telescope. Both magnify but in different ways.

A microscope magnifies a smaller object making it appear bigger. As we glorify the Lord, we're like a microscope because even though he may be regarded as "small" (impotent and untrustworthy) by others, our responses cause him to appear "bigger" (powerful, real, and loving).

Paul writes: *it is my eager expectation and hope that I will not be at all ashamed, but that with full courage now as always Christ will be honored in my body, whether by life or by death* (Philippians 1:20). The word "honored" is also translated "magnified" and "exalted."

Likewise, the telescope magnifies a distant object as clearer and nearer. As we respond in life to difficult situations or face challenging people with bold love, patience, and wisdom, we will clarify God's holy nature before the eyes of others. No, not perfectly. But we will credit God with any loving or courageous reactions beyond our own ability.

Confidence in his empowering comes from his assurance he wants us to reflect him. God says: *So I will show my greatness and my holiness and make myself known in the eyes of many nations. Then they will know that I am the Lord* (Ezekiel 38:23).

In the summer of 2013, I could see the flames and smoke from a forest fire in the mountains near Idyllwild, California, sixty miles away from us. We were totally safe from the danger but our friends,

Robin and Karen Wood, who founded and run Camp Alandale, a Christian camp for abused children, were not. Karen posted a God-glorifying note on Facebook early that morning:

> Last night was the first night we saw a glow from the fire from our vantage point. We had only seen billowing smoke and ashes before. This weekend will be the climax of the fight due to the expected rain storm. We are about eight miles from the fire's location and it'll hit Idyllwild first because it's only two miles from the fire. If the embers escape the firefighters' best efforts, the fire will descend into Idyllwild and its surrounding communities. It is truly in God's hands and that makes it peacefully acceptable for whatever happens. Our camp belongs to God and can be done anywhere. I can't imagine we will lose camp but we are prepared to move out where God leads. I mourn for the children who will be disappointed if we have to cancel camps for the rest of the summer. I rejoice that our lives have never been dull and uneventful!

A little while later, Karen sent an email saying they had been ordered to leave their home and for the remaining staff to leave the camp grounds. She closed her note with James 1:2-4: *Count it all joy, my brothers, when you meet trials of various kinds, for you know that the testing of your faith produces steadfastness. And let steadfastness have its full effect, that you may be perfect and complete, lacking in nothing.*

Karen was making God look good, magnifying him before others.

Can There Be Too Much Heart Evaluation?

"Pure-Hearted" was the theme of a retreat where I was speaking (different from the retreat at this chapter's beginning). At Saturday evening's dinner, I sat with several women including the pastor's wife. We chatted back and forth about evaluating our motives. I gave an example where I reacted in an ungodly way and then questioned myself about what had been going on in my heart. As a result, I identified I wanted to be seen as dependable by others or else I felt worthless. I wasn't concerned about what God thought of me—only other people.

As I shared, I could tell the pastor's wife seemed a little antsy. She spoke up saying, "Well, I'm sure Kathy doesn't evaluate herself nonstop. We shouldn't only be focused on ourselves." I could understand her concern thinking those listening would only focus on themselves and not reach out to others until they had perfect motives.

When she turned to me for my agreement, I knew I had a heart challenge for myself. *I better not risk displeasing her because she could be a source for future ministry opportunities, even holding my reputation in her hands.*

But, I knew I wouldn't be trusting God. He prompted me within to be truthful and clarify. So, I replied, "Well, actually, in the beginning of my journey in evaluating my motives, it did feel like I evaluated everything. I believed it necessary to get in touch with my heart. But now I can more quickly identify my primary triggers." I went on to explain how I could now respond to the needs of others more lovingly and obey God more regularly.

I felt relieved when the pastor's wife said she agreed. Even if she hadn't, I could keep my eyes on Jesus because he can fulfill his will for my ministry or my impact in whatever ways he desires.

The Biblical Basis for Heart Evaluation

There are many biblical passages encouraging us to evaluate our hearts—our motives. The one most often quoted is Proverbs 16:2: *All the ways of a man are clean in his own sight, But the Lord weighs the motives.*

James, the half-brother of Jesus, encourages us to avoid deceiving ourselves. *But be doers of the word, and not hearers only, deceiving yourselves. For if anyone is a hearer of the word and not a doer, he is like a man who looks intently at his natural face in a mirror. For he looks at himself and goes away and at once forgets what he was like* (James 1:22-24).

The two words "looks intently" in the Greek can be defined as bending over for the purpose of intensely looking, focused on satisfying one's curiosity. Such intense scrutiny implies intentionality. Jeremiah 17:9-10 says why:

> The heart is deceitful above all things, and desperately sick; who can understand it? "I the Lord search the heart and test the mind, to give every man according to his ways, according to the fruit of his deeds.

Being open to God searching our hearts will help us fulfill the admonition of Ephesians 5:10: *try to discern what is pleasing to the Lord.* From numerous passages in the Bible, we find out what pleases God's heart and glorifies him to others. We learn he doesn't expect us to have perfect motives but to be purifying our hearts.

Such purification is a continual journey motivated by knowing there will be an accounting. *Therefore do not pronounce judgment before the time, before the Lord comes, who will bring to light the things now hidden in darkness and will disclose the purposes of the heart. Then each one will receive his commendation from God* (I Corinthians 4:5).

This "commendation" doesn't determine our salvation, which we address in Chapter 4. But here on earth, we can easily deceive ourselves thinking we're fooling everyone with "good" choices fueled by sinful motives. People may be misled but God isn't. How God will highlight our earthly choices in heaven I do not know, but regardless of rewards or not, we can want to concentrate today on bringing glory to God. Jude 24-25 assures us where our transformation comes from.

> Now to him who is able to keep you from stumbling and to present you blameless before the presence of his glory with great joy, to the only God, our Savior, through Jesus Christ our Lord, be glory, majesty, dominion, and authority, before all time and now and forever. Amen.

With all this in mind, listen to the experience of psychologist and author of *Loveable*, Dr. Kelly Flanagan.

> Earlier this year, our family was preparing to embark upon an adventure, picking up our lives and plopping them back down in a new town and a new culture. It seemed grand and epic, but it began with a lot of tedium. Like replacing the carpet in the bedroom.

> Our realtor said we needed new rugs so we called the rug people. The morning they arrived, we thought we were taking a big step toward where we wanted to go, but it came to a screeching halt when they pulled back a corner of the carpet.

> Asbestos.

It was another hurdle and it was expensive and it slowed us down, so it was a little frustrating. But even more so, it was a little disorienting. We'd been walking on a toxin for six years and hadn't known it. It was a little concerning that something so important existed just beneath the surface of our life.

Disorienting and concerning, but not unfamiliar.

Because I'm a therapist and, at the beginning, that's exactly how therapy can feel.

We usually go to therapy for help with a specific problem, like dirty carpet we can see and want to remove. But, inevitably, we start to pull it up, and we find stuff underneath we didn't know existed. Stuff that's a little more complicated, a little more frustrating, probably even a little more painful.

Therapy doesn't create it; therapy reveals it.

We sense this might be true, and so we avoid the endeavor altogether. We decide to live with the dirty carpet, or we put on blindfolds and try to replace the carpet ourselves, without looking at what's beneath it. Yet, there comes a time for some of us when we decide we're ready to lift up the carpet and face the unknown.[5]

I can understand if Dr. Flanagan's words aren't thrilling. Yes, the pool of murky motives underneath "the carpet" seems daunting and it may even feel like the muddy water is up to your chin, but with God's help, you and I can purify our desires and grow through seeking God's glory. We may not know exactly what giving glory to God looks like each day but we'll trust he does and will fulfill it.

Knowing he desires only what's best for us can give us confidence in his work. May I say it this way? Our almighty God's motives are to purify us with a gentle touch to use us for his glory.

Salome
Matthew 20:20-24

Imagine for a moment your own sons are disciples of Jesus. What an honor, for certainly they are followers of the future king of Israel, who will overthrow the Roman tyranny. And what does a king need? Advisors sitting beside him ... well ... advising him. Wouldn't any mother think *My sons can do that. They're brilliant.*

Yes, we're using our imagination. And in our imagination, wouldn't it be possible (as our sons sit on the platform near the king, and we stand on the sidelines of the great hall), we would whisper to the woman next to us, "See those two right there near the king? Those are my sons."

This fictional example is based on the story of Salome, the mother of the sons of Zebedee, James and John. By connecting Matthew 27:55-56 and Mark 15:40, we know she is the one referred to in Matthew 20:20-24. Let's read the story.

> Then the mother of the sons of Zebedee came up to him with her sons, and kneeling before him she asked him for something. And he said to her, "What do you want?" She said to him, "Say that these two sons of mine are to sit, one at your right hand and one at your left, in your kingdom." Jesus answered, "You do not know what you are asking. Are you able to drink the cup that I am to drink?" They said to him, "We are able." He said to them, "You will drink my cup, but to sit at my right hand and at my left is not mine to grant, but it is for those for whom it has been prepared by my Father." And when the ten heard it, they were indignant at the two brothers. Matthew 20:20-24

Of course, we don't know Salome's thoughts, but from the biblical story, it would seem she had high hopes for them. Who could fault Salome's motives in wanting the best for her precious boys?

Yet Salome's heart may have impure motives. At least, she has faith to believe Jesus will be king. We don't know if she envisions an earthly or a heavenly kingdom with Jesus as king. Regardless, she is asking for something seemingly right, yet she doesn't recognize her heart is muddied by the idea of her sons' future status and success. Little does she know what she is asking, as Jesus points out. And little did she anticipate the indignation of the other ten disciples. She hadn't expected that. Unfortunately, our mixed motives often block out the potential consequences of our choices.

Thankfully, we know Salome stayed faithful to Jesus and was one of the three women standing together at the cross of Jesus (Matthew 27:55-56 and Mark 15:40-41). Even if her hopes of her sons' status died there, we also know from Mark 16:1-8 Salome was one of three women who went to the tomb to anoint Jesus' body with spices. She saw the angel and the empty tomb. How her heart must have leaped with joy. I doubt by then she was thinking of her sons' status. I'd like to think she could only think of Jesus being glorified.

That's the challenge for each one of us. To allow the loving Father to bring glory to himself through purifying our hearts.

Reflection and Discussion Questions

1. What drew you to this book?

2. What do you hope to gain?

3. How would you have defined "motive" before reading this chapter? Has your definition changed?

4. How do you feel thinking of blessings in conection with wanting God's glory?

5. How have you thought of God's glory in the past? How would you define it now?

6. Can you share a time when you thought your motives were pure yet realized later they weren't quite as pure as you'd thought?

7. In what way do you think Jesus most glorified his Father?

8. Of the nine blessings, which one seems most uncharacteristic of you now? Which one seems most evident in your choices?

9. How do you feel thinking of evaluating your heart's motives? What is scary? What is inviting?

10. What do you think examining your heart's motives might bring?

11. What was your reaction to Dr. Flanagan's story?

12. What are you afraid you might discover under your soul's "carpet"? What are you hoping to find?

Chapter 2
Selflessness
Love Others Well

To "love" the person in front of me does not mean I necessarily feel warm and fuzzy toward them, or that it's my job to make them feel good (even worse, to like me). "Love" is simply engaging my will for another person's good.[6]—Jan Johnson

There will be no lasting growth in godliness if we fail to expose the sinful longings of the heart (what truly motivates us) and thus identify what it is we crave so badly that we are willing to disobey God in order to get it.[7]—Paul Tautges

Whenever we visited Larry's parents, Don and Audrey, the issue of Larry's weight always came up. Although far from heavy, if Larry carried some extra weight, Audrey warned him, "Larry, you know we have diabetes in our family. It's only because your dad stays thin he doesn't take medicine. Get your weight down."

Larry would shrug his shoulders. "OK, mom."

Unlike Larry, my mother-in-law's warnings grated on my nerves for I knew when we finished eating, Audrey would see the remaining mashed potatoes, grab the dish, and push the remainder onto Larry's plate. "We can't waste this. Eat it." And he would.

I sat fuming. *Didn't you just tell him earlier he should watch his weight?*

Every time we visited, the scenario flummoxed me. *Why can't she see how she's not loving Larry well?*

Not until many years later did I figure out Audrey's motivation.

Audrey was raised in the Depression by a single mom. Her dad died when Audrey was five years old. No one wasted anything. Larry and I became convinced Audrey must have been shamed about wasting something. As a result, she and Don, also raised in the Depression by a single mom, counted every penny.

Only when we could identify Audrey's fear of being shamed for wasting did we understand her motive. She wasn't loving Larry well, and yet she would have passionately claimed she loved him with a pure heart. I felt grieved thinking of her wounded heart.

The Selflessness of Loving *Well*

For several years I've become more aware of the important phrase *loving well*. We often believe we're loving others but using the word "well" puts an important emphasis upon the quality of our love—and the motivation for the choices we make.

Paul stresses in Romans 15:1-2, 3, 5-7:

We who are strong have an obligation to bear with the failings of the weak, and not to please ourselves. Let each of us please his neighbor for his good, to build him up. For Christ did not please himself, but as it is written, 'The reproaches of those who reproached you fell on me.' May the God of endurance and encouragement grant you to live in such harmony with one another, in accord with Christ Jesus, that together you may with one voice glorify the God and Father of our Lord Jesus Christ. Therefore welcome one another as Christ has welcomed you, for the glory of God.

Paul defined loving well as choosing another person's good empowered by wanting God's glory. The more we want God glorified, the more we'll be able to love others even to the point of sacrificing our own needs and desires. Jesus said: *By this all people will know that you are my disciples, if you have love for one another* (John 13:35). Jesus chose that particular response—love—as the primary characteristic of showing our connection to him. He could have chosen gentleness, wisdom, trusting God, or any number of characteristics.

He chose love. Why? Love is how God describes his essence. The apostle John wrote God is love (1 John 4:8) and his whole first epistle is primarily about love—God's love through his Son Jesus Christ and how we should love others. When we love well, Jesus' own love is made more apparent to the world. As a result, we give him glory.

Mixed Motives

Paul wrote the famous "love chapter" (I Corinthians 13:1-3), which begins:

If I speak in the tongues of men and of angels, but have not love, I am a noisy gong or a clanging cymbal. And if I have prophetic powers, and understand all mysteries and all knowledge, and if I have all faith, so as to remove mountains, but have not love, I am nothing. If I give away all I have, and if I deliver up my body to be burned, but have not love, I gain nothing.

These verses have everything to do with motive. We can reach out, sacrifice, spend all our time, spend all our money, and believe we are obeying God yet we might not be energized by love. Paul challenges us to be aware of our motives.

Jesus emphasized the heart's motives in the Sermon on the Mount.

You have heard that it was said to those of old, "You shall not murder; and whoever murders will be liable to judgment.'" But I say to you that everyone who is angry with his brother will be liable to judgment; whoever insults his brother will be liable to the council; and whoever says, "You fool!" will be liable to the hell of fire. Matthew 5:21-22

God doesn't judge only the extreme motive resulting in murder. If our motive is to hurt in any way, we desire someone's harm. Insulting a brother or calling someone a fool shows our heart's intention. We are rejecting God's call to love them well for his glory. We can't say, "I didn't kill them, after all. I only intended to get their attention, or change them, or take revenge" or ... your motive of choice. The heart with wrong motives is guilty of sin against God.

Jesus emphasized this because the Jewish spiritual "guides" said the sixth commandment—*you shall not murder* (Exodus 20:13)—only referred to actual murder. Jesus stressed the heart's motives and therefore "murder" is defined in Matthew 5 and 6 as anything not for another's good to fulfill our own selfish needs.

Selfishness can be expressed in a variety of ways. Anger "kills" another person's sense of freedom because they are afraid to act.

"Insulting" is from the Greek word *raca* and reveals contempt, indicating another person is worthless. The word "fool" is based in hating someone, thus saying they are not worthy of being treated well. Yet God loves and values every person because he created each one in his image. We are never "worthy" of receiving anything good, but we do have worth and value in God's sight.

A few verses later, Jesus again points out mixed motives. *You have heard that it was said, "You shall not commit adultery." But I say to you that everyone who looks at a woman with lustful intent has already committed adultery with her in his heart* (vss. 27-28).

It's not just what we in reality do, but what we imagine and fantasize.

Then Jesus points out other "opportunities" revealing our heart's impulses. *Beware of practicing your righteousness before other people in order to be seen by them, for then you will have no reward from your Father who is in heaven* (6:1).

We can act right and possibly receive public acclaim, but we can't expect eternal rewards if empowered by self-glory. Jesus isn't requiring perfection, but the more we're aware of what's going on in our hearts, the more we're open to God's purifying.

If we do receive public acclaim, we don't need to shun it. It may be God's encouraging gift. But our primary goal should be hearing from God: *Well done, good and faithful servant* (Matthew 25:23). When we receive appreciation from others, we can express our gratitude and refer to God's empowering. Rejecting the comment only draws more attention to ourselves.

In the next verses, Jesus says the same thing is true about giving to the needy (vss. 2-4), praying (vss. 5-6), and fasting (vss. 16-18). Jesus tells us self-absorbed motivations cause us to become hypocrites. The word "hypocrite" originally referred to actors wearing masks to play different parts on the stage. We're on the stage of life hoping we'll receive a standing ovation.

Jesus continues his sermon saying: *The eye is the lamp of the body. So, if your eye is healthy, your whole body will be full of light, but if your eye is bad, your whole body will be full of darkness. If then the light in you is darkness, how great is the darkness!* (vss. 22-23).

The *Jamieson-Fausset-Brown Bible Commentary* gives this explanation: "As applied to the outward eye, this means general soundness; particularly, not looking two ways. Here, as also in classical Greek, it is used figuratively to denote the simplicity of the mind's eye, singleness of purpose, looking right at its object, as opposed to having two ends in view."[8]

The "eye" represents our perspective, motive, and desires forming the foundation of our behavior. God wants us to experience the peace of being single-minded and having a pure heart.

Jesus concludes: *No one can serve two masters, for either he will hate the one and love the other, or he will be devoted to the one and despise the other* (vs. 24). As we grow in pure heartedness, we'll have more of a single focus by serving the only true Master there is.

What Motivates Our Motives?

We desire to serve only one master but our behavior betrays us. We sigh, calling out, "I want to love well and be selfless. I want God's glory, but selfishness keeps creeping in. Why? What motivates my motivations?"

I hear you. I've exclaimed those very words. I'm not trying to make you feel hopeless. Just the opposite. We cannot begin to more often respond with love for another's good unless we first recognize the need for growth. If you feel distressed, you are in a good place. Your heart is hungry for change and he promises to respond (Proverbs 2:1-5).

If we ask for understanding, God will reveal the core of our actions: whether our motives are murky or pure. Pure motives are fueled by the right kind of fear—reverence and submission—along with knowing God in truth. Most importantly, he truly does love us and wants the best for us as Philippians 4:19 promises. *And my God will supply every need of yours according to his riches in glory in Christ Jesus.*

Let me say it clearly. In the moment we react out of impure motives, we are not trusting God's perfect love. That truth is not meant to discourage us but to draw us closer to him. We can reverse disbelief by learning more and more of his motive to supply what's best. Then we can pass along such love to others unselfishly.

Isaiah's Story

The story of Isaiah's encounter with a holy God speaks volumes of how God loves well and wants us to love well without expectation of a return. The story starts with Isaiah standing in the presence of a holy God (Isaiah 6). He is completely overwhelmed with sorrow as he faces his sin. He confesses, and God supplies forgiveness and purification through a seraphim touching a burning coal to Isaiah's mouth.

Completely humbled, Isaiah is shocked to hear God's invitation: *Whom shall I send, and who will go for us?* Isaiah volunteers *Here I am! Send me* (vs. 8). In response, God basically explains, "Go love these people by sharing my message but don't expect to be loved back. They won't respond. So, don't expect any feedback to encourage you, any gratitude to support you, any praise to empower you. I, only, will know and appreciate what you're doing. I am the only one who will provide everything you need. Keep your eyes on me."

Isaiah must have gulped, yet spoke up, *How long, O Lord?* (6:11). Isaiah must have gulped again when God explains the people will never be responsive. Did Isaiah want to take back his offer?

Do we? Yet God wants us to represent his glory by loving others with no assurance of applause, approval, or acknowledgment.

The more we can accept this commission with no assurance of having our own needs met, the more we can love others *well*. The more we can know God is approving us, the more we can love others *well*. The more we accept the assignment as intended to bring God glory, the more we can love others *well*.

A Choice Among Many

We don't know whether Isaiah had a choice. You and I do have choices when it comes to being selfless. The problem is we often don't recognize there's more than one choice. For instance, consider:

Our adult child is addicted to drugs. What other choice could there be but to pay for rehab? That's the way to force him to change.

Our hung-over husband is unable to go to work. What other choice could there be but to call in to say he's got a migraine? The family needs him to work.

Our friend complains about another friend's mistreatment. What other choice could there be but to tell her she's always right and the other friend always wrong? Her side of the conflict makes it clear.

In situations like these, we can't imagine any other way to love but the obvious. And what we've always done. Still, such choices may not be loving others well. Our goal is to protect others from pain and be seen in a positive light. Yet, we are convinced we are giving God glory.

I recently met Lydia at a women's conference. She explained she'd recently moved closer to her son and his family. The peace and calm she expected had exploded in her face. His wife moved out to live with her boyfriend, whom no one knew about. Lydia was now needed full time to care for the children and tend to her son's emotional turmoil.

Her voice became tense. "I didn't move here to be a caregiver; I moved here to have fun with my grandchildren. Now I have to discipline them. They don't like me anymore."

Lydia explained, "I moved away from my daughter and her family. I just couldn't handle my daughter's chaotic life any longer. I had no peace there. I was expected to come through for her and my grandchildren."

Since I'd been sharing the principles of this book, I asked her, "What was your motive to move closer to your other grandchildren?"

"Well, like I told you, I just wanted to be a fun grandma and …"

Suddenly, she stopped as tears came to her eyes. "Oh … maybe it wasn't just about being a fun grandma but getting away from the chaos of my daughter's life."

She wiped her cheeks and stared at me. "Now, instead of the peace and quiet I expected, I'm right back into the sizzling pan."

I gently asked her, "Did God direct you to move?"

"Well, of course, what else would …"

She seemed to shrink. "I guess I really didn't ask. It just seemed like a loving thing to do … be there as the fun grandma. I guess my real motive was to escape the chaos and be loved as the fun grandma."

God revealed her motives of protecting herself from pain by using the unexpected chaos of her son's life.

After we prayed together, Lydia murmured, "I guess God wants me to find my peace in him, and then, I'll be able to love them well."

Like my new friend, we often aren't aware of our motives. We might even claim we're loving others for God's glory. God may decide to use surprises to help us identify our hidden selfish motives—if we can be honest.

Resist Hurt Feelings

Pastor Tim Keller writes, "People sometimes say their feelings are hurt. But our feelings can't be hurt! It is the ego that hurts—my sense of self, my identity. Our feelings are fine! It is my ego that hurts."[9]

Is Pastor Keller's perspective difficult to receive or even understand? I understand! I have a long history of being easily offended. I felt justified to react with criticism, anger, and manipulation if others seemed to indicate I was imperfect, incapable, or unloving. I didn't recognize I gave another person the key to my heart's condition.

Now, I know I can bring glory to God by seeing the truth: being offended blocks my ability to see their motives to protect themselves. Their comments say less about me than it does their emotional wounds and needs.

When Larry and I were at odds with each other after seven years of marriage, I was furious at him for not meeting my needs. I believed his lack of care communicated I was unimportant. Of all people, he was supposed to be the one telling me I was important. My anger was my "means" of saying he had offended me. He hurt my feelings! When he wasn't motivated to change, I felt even more unimportant.

What I didn't realize was my "offense" blocked me from seeing his needs. I could only focus on my needs. I wasn't loving him well because I thought if I stopped being angry, I would be exposed to more rejection. I didn't look to God to be my defender and refuge. And of course, I had no thought of God's glory.

In turn, my anger gave Larry the impression he could never satisfy me and that he was a failure as a husband. To protect himself from feeling weak and powerless, he not only resisted but actively avoided interaction with me. When he did interact with me, I complained and pointed out all the ways he wasn't being "good" to me.

As a result, he worked more—as a policeman, a real estate agent, and flying a plane as a hobby. He wanted to avoid feeling like a failure, and I wanted to avoid feeling unloved. God wasn't glorified as I whined, complained, and criticized my husband to any friend who would listen.

In time, God graciously healed us, but we didn't fully understand our motives. God was faithful to bring healing because our restoration would glorify himself.

Who is reacting to you in a "hurtful" way? Have you considered their motives? Have you considered their hurting heart? Through your reactions, you may be telling them lies they will try to avoid at all costs. You are not responsible for their reactions, but you are responsible before God to love them well by seeing them through God's eyes of love. Then your love will honor God. And like Isaiah, serve others without any demand to have your love returned.

The next time you are tempted to be selfish, ask God to reveal if feeling offended or blaming others is involved. If so, you may be trying to avoid taking responsibility for your own choices.

Evaluate Your Expectations

Jesus always responded out of realistic expectations. He knew the heart of man. *But Jesus on his part did not entrust himself to them, because he knew all people* (John 2:24). When we have expectations, in a sense we are "entrusting ourselves to them." We're saying, "Come through for me; I need this and you hold the key to my need." When someone doesn't, we might have a difficult time loving them well and understanding why they didn't—or couldn't.

Jesus knew those who resisted him had hard hearts. He knew his disciples would be inadequate, even though he was the perfect teacher and mentor. Jesus didn't expect Peter to be perfect. He knew Peter would reject him three times, which he didn't prevent. Jesus knew the heart of man, and he only valued his Father's opinion of him and his work. Jesus could love Peter well later by offering forgiveness and restoration. God received more glory through Jesus' expression of unconditional love for Peter.

What are you expecting people to provide for you which only God can and should provide? You will be able to love others well by recognizing they are wounded themselves.

Allow Consequences

When we think of loving someone, it's just "natural" to want them to enjoy life, avoid difficulty, and be happy. And doesn't being "happy" mean valuing themselves, loving their life, and having good self-esteem? After all, God is the giver of every good thing, even Jesus's half-brother James says so. *Every good gift and every perfect gift is from above, coming down from the Father of lights with whom there is no variation or shadow due to change* (1:7).

When our loved one experiences roadblocks, his prayers aren't answered "yes," or he says God failed him, we want to shield, provide solutions, and protect from consequences. It's hard for us to thank and trust God. We can even become angry and bitter.

But ask yourself: I wonder if thanking God for my loved one's problem is the most God-honoring response I can choose? I wonder if allowing them to suffer is really for their best? I wonder if it's the way for me to love them *well*? Seem impossible?

God the Father loved his only Son well to the maximum but still asked Jesus to leave heaven's joys to demonstrate the Father's love for sinful humanity. *All for the sake of bringing glory to the Father.* God also suffered himself watching his beloved Son suffer. He provided darkness to cover his Son's unbearable pain on the cross.

The physical suffering Jesus endured wasn't the most painful aspect of his crucifixion. No, the most painful and important aspect was the indescribable emotional agony Jesus suffered by being separated from his Father's fellowship. They had never been separated before. God the Father, Jesus the Son, and the Holy Spirit had always enjoyed perfect fellowship, unity, and joy in each other. When Jesus took on the sins of the world, though he had lived a sinless life, he became sinful which separated him from perfect fellowship in the holy Trinity. The ultimate suffering was *that* separation and being burdened with every sin of every human being when he didn't deserve any of it. God's heart was grieved yet he had a purpose in Jesus' crucifixion.

I can't imagine any of us willing to send our beloved husband, child, or friend to a cross. But we don't have to willingly send anyone into difficulty. We're all challenged more than enough because we're part of this sinful world, yet God knows his purpose to purify through those trials. Cooperation with God's purposes means to resist protecting and rescuing others, and especially excusing their sinful choices.

Think of James 1:2-5. We find great comfort and power from this passage for ourselves when we are in difficult circumstances:

Count it all joy, my brothers, when you meet trials of various kinds, for you know that the testing of your faith produces steadfastness. And let steadfastness have its full effect, that you may be perfect and complete, lacking in nothing. If any of you lacks wisdom, let him ask God, who gives generously to all without reproach, and it will be given him.

Recently, I meditated on those verses from a different angle. When I try to protect or rescue anyone I love, in a sense I'm standing before God exclaiming, "You may not speak James 1:2-5 to him. You may not challenge him to count it all joy. It's just too much for me to think of him suffering. You aren't capable of using this situation for his good. Having you glorified through his difficulties is not as valuable to me as his comfort and ease."

Are you shocked to think of it that way?

Here's something even more shocking. In a sense we're demanding, "You must remove those verses from the Bible. They aren't true."

Shocking, yes, but we deceive ourselves thinking shielding them is for their best. God doesn't agree. He loves each one of us perfectly well, and yet he says, *Count it all joy*. Why? Because then, as the passage says, the payoff is strength, steadfastness, wisdom, growth, and maturity.

Aren't those qualities what you desire for your beloved? Only God's use of difficulty will produce those benefits.

Am I saying we never help or assist or advise or support? Absolutely not. But we must be honest about our motives in order to know what's best for them. Sometimes we don't want them to suffer because it hurts us to see their pain. Desiring God's glory clears up our muddy motives.

Keep in mind rescuing can set up a repeating cycle. Proverbs 19:19 warns us: *A man of great wrath will pay the penalty, for if you deliver him, you will only have to do it again.* In the NASB, that word "deliver" is translated "rescue."

You can substitute any sin or temptation for "great wrath": addiction, turning from God, being apathetic toward God, making unwise choices, marrying an unbeliever, or whatever our loved one is choosing. If we try to interject ourselves in any way, leaving out trust in God, we are most likely going to have to deliver and rescue again and again.

Sometimes we feel compelled to jump into trying to rescue, direct, manipulate, or other ungodly and unloving reactions because we fear erring on the side of doing too little. But isn't God capable of providing what is needed? Isn't he capable of bringing alongside assistance? We are not the "great gap substitute." We may try to be because our motive is to avoid others' criticism who say we aren't doing "enough."

As soon as we think we're the answer to another person's problems or act out of fear, our motives are revealed. We think we are the solution. We aren't trusting God. The degree to which we love selflessly and without fear is the degree to which we trust and love God.

A Word of Reason

When I encourage us to love selflessly, I'm not saying we should never take care of ourselves. We should seek God to know how he defines "selfless" in each area of our lives.

By following his Father's direction, Jesus took good care of himself. Luke 5:15-16 shares an interesting peek into Jesus' choices. *But now even more the report about him went abroad, and great crowds gathered to hear him and to be healed of their infirmities. But he would withdraw to desolate places and pray.*

Imagine the scene. Great crowds gathered surrounding Jesus with great needs. They wanted out of their pain. Then Jesus walked away. Just walked away. And his purpose—to take care of himself through prayer.

How they must have grumbled. "He says he's God, but he didn't heal *me*! He talks about love. That's not loving us!"

Jesus risked his very reputation—and his Father's—to do what was right for himself. He wasn't held hostage by the expectations of others. Let God define "selflessness" for you.

Love Well; God Loves You Well

Our fourth wedding anniversary approached, June 20, and I was pregnant. I felt undesirable with the added weight and morning sickness. *If Larry buys me flowers, then I'll really know he still loves me.* I knew Larry didn't value buying me flowers, but my heart argued, *He should know how important this is to me.*

Getting flowers wasn't the only thing I anticipated. We'd decided to build a pool in the backyard, and I was excited to think we could be swimming in a few short weeks.

June 20 finally arrived. Unexpectedly, the doorbell rang. I opened the door to find a delivery boy holding a gorgeous spray of red roses in a vase. "Larry does love me. He actually thought of flowers himself!"

I eagerly opened the card anticipating the romantic words Larry wrote. Instead, I read "Congratulations on choosing us to build your new pool. We know you'll love it!" signed by the pool company.

Suddenly, I started laughing. I had built up my expectations of receiving love from Larry through flowers. Instead, I'd received roses from a pool company. How like the Lord.

Lord, you orchestrated these flowers to arrive on my anniversary so I wouldn't be disappointed when Larry arrives home empty-handed. You love me well.

That example of God's provision stands out in my memory building my faith in God's ability to meet my true needs. I'm still selfish often, but I'm more able to choose selflessness as I trust God more and more to meet my true needs.

The next time you are tempted to be selfish and protect yourself or others from pain, remember how God has loved you well. You'll find yourself wanting to honor and give God glory.

The Syrophoenician Woman
Matthew 15:21-28

We don't know her name yet she is applauded in biblical history as a woman who loved well. She loved selflessly because she trusted Jesus by being willing to be misunderstood.

And Jesus went away from there and withdrew to the district of Tyre and Sidon. And behold, a Canaanite woman from that region came out and was crying, "Have mercy on me, O Lord, Son of David; my daughter is severely oppressed by a demon." But he did not answer her a word. And his disciples came and begged him, saying, "Send her away, for she is crying out after us." He answered, "I was sent only to the lost sheep of the house of Israel." But she came and knelt before him, saying, "Lord, help me." And he answered, "It is not right to take the children's bread and throw it to the dogs." She said, "Yes, Lord, yet even the dogs eat the crumbs that fall from their masters' table." Then Jesus answered her, "O woman, great is your faith! Be it done for you as you desire." And her daughter was healed instantly. Matthew 15:21-28

Slow the story down and think about this woman, this mom.

She humbles herself for the sake of her daughter by begging. Her faith believed Jesus could heal even though many others may have promised to help.

She *perseveres.* Both the disciples and Jesus himself put up roadblocks. Yet she doesn't give up.

She discounts the bullying of others. She doesn't allow a personal assault to slow down her motivation to love her daughter well. Of course, we don't know, but the fact she is not accompanied by a husband or any man may mean she is a single mom.

She wisely responds. Jesus enjoys engaging her knowing her intelligence and strength. In a sense, he includes her in the process of developing her faith.

She believes her request is answered. She left the scene with no guarantee Jesus had done what he said, but he had (Mark 7:30).

Whether you are seeking to give God glory through loving well your child, husband, friend, co-worker, or enemy, be assured God wants to empower you. He loves you so much—you have plenty to give away. Trust him to provide all you need for then you can abundantly share.

Reflection and Discussion Questions

1. Can you identify one or more sinful motivations which you hadn't recognized before? How does that motivation leave out trust in God?

2. Can you pinpoint another person's motive which you hadn't identified before?

3. Which concept from this chapter made the greatest impact on you?

4. Can you think of a time when you thought you knew someone's motives but it turned out you were wrong? Describe.

5. Does the concept of loving *well* make a difference in your thinking?

6. Which Scripture verse(s) was most important to you from this chapter?

7. What did you think about Isaiah's encounter with God? Explain how if it was meaningful.

8. Who have you depended upon to feel loved? How has that turned out?

9. When you've tried to love someone but they didn't appreciate it, how did you respond? What do you want to do in a similar situation in the future?

10. Describe how these statements may seem true but they are lies:

   • I have only one choice in how to respond to a person:

   • What others do define me:

   • I'm entitled to have expectations, even if they are unrealistic:

11. Can you describe a time you didn't allow consequences for another? And/or a time you did allow consequences?

12. What impacted you about the Syrophoenician Woman?

Chapter 3
Surrender
Trusting God's Plan

This fallen nature in us believes that we're smarter than God. I've never met anyone who will say that, but I've met hundreds of people who live like that: "I'm smarter than God[10].—Matt Chandler

When you say that you are waiting, that means that you are accepting God's wise timing. You are confessing, 'I'm not fussing. I'm not fuming. I'm not fixing.[11]—James McDonald

It just didn't make sense to me. If God would only instantly wipe away my anger, he would receive glory and I wouldn't be a disastrous example of a Christian. I was twenty-seven years old, had been a Christian for ten years, and I was abusing our two-year-old daughter.

My constant prayer was, "Lord, take away my anger! I don't want to be like this."

When my angry responses increased in occurrence and intensity, I felt abandoned. *God doesn't love me. Why isn't he helping me? Wouldn't it be most glorious to God if I could say, "God instantaneously delivered me from abusive anger! Glory to God!"?*

All of us face times when God's plan doesn't seem to bring God maximum glory. Surrendering because we trust him is extremely challenging. At times, he seems to delay his plan, and other times, he works in a different way than expected. Each challenge is an opportunity to examine our motives, surrender more and believe he will bring glory to himself.

Surrender Admits God Is Smarter Than Me

Even the idea we would think of being smarter than God Almighty seems ridiculous. Yet our lack of trust is saying exactly that. Listen to Job:

Behold, I cry out, 'Violence!' but I am not answered;
I call for help, but there is no justice. Job 19:7

In another place, he cries out:

Oh, that I had one to hear me!
(Here is my signature! Let the Almighty answer me!)
Oh, that I had the indictment written by my adversary!
Surely I would carry it on my shoulder;
I would bind it on me as a crown;
I would give him an account of all my steps;
like a prince I would approach him. 31:35-37

Job's saying, "God, you don't know what you're doing but I do!" His motive is to be proven righteous and vindicated before his friends.

In time, God does answer Job and says:

Then the Lord answered Job out of the whirlwind and said:
'Who is this that darkens counsel by words without knowledge?
Dress for action like a man;
I will question you, and you make it known to me.
"Where were you when I laid the foundation of the earth?
Tell me, if you have understanding.
Who determined its measurements—surely you know!
Or who stretched the line upon it?
On what were its bases sunk,
or who laid its cornerstone,
when the morning stars sang together
and all the sons of God shouted for joy? 38:1-7

God is basically saying, "If you're so smart, why don't you tell me how I created the universe?"

Surrender Doesn't Grumble

When we think we're smarter than God, we grumble and dispute, basically indicating we think God is doing a lousy job. We may think we're just grumbling against the stupidity of others, but God has allowed their "stupidity," therefore, ultimately, we are grumbling against him. He is sovereign. He could change a person or a circumstance. Yet he hasn't.

Let's look at Mark 6:30-36.

The apostles returned to Jesus and told him all that they had done and taught. And he said to them, 'Come away by yourselves to a desolate place and rest a while.' For many were coming and going, and they had no leisure even to eat. And they went away in the boat to a desolate place by themselves. Now many saw them going and recognized them, and they ran there on foot from all the towns and got there ahead of them. When he went ashore he saw a great crowd, and he had compassion on them, because they were like sheep without a shepherd. And he began to teach them many things. And when it grew late, his disciples came to him and said, 'This is a desolate place, and the hour is now late. Send them away to go into the surrounding countryside and villages and buy themselves something to eat.' But he answered them, 'You give them something to eat.' And they said to him, 'Shall we go and buy two hundred denarii worth of bread and give it to them to eat?'

The disciples had just returned from a very successful evangelistic campaign and they were exhausted. Time alone with Jesus without all these needy people? Priceless!

But the silly crowd runs to meet them. The disciples' hope of rest is dashed. They know Jesus will react with compassion. Just like him. *Now we won't get what we need. What about our needs?*

How could they subtly communicate their displeasure, yet hide their heart's motive? Grumble. "Jesus, send them away. Tell them to leave us alone. Let's go back to the original plan of rest."

Of course, I could be wrong about their tone and their motive but notice their next words of exaggerated sarcasm: "Oh, OK, Jesus, I suppose you want us to go buy food with money we don't have. Do you realize how much it's going to cost?" They can't seem to trust Jesus' heart of love.

I have no right to be critical of the disciples. I've been in their shoes, er, sandals. I've been weary "serving the Lord." I've grumbled in my heart. "God! Acknowledge my sacrifice for your sake." Or "Stop mistreating me." Can I say that outright to him? No, because grumbling sounds so unspiritual and I think I must be seen as the spiritual person. But my heart feels uncared for and my motive is to protect myself from feeling unlovable.

We mask our uncertainty of God's care and love, not by honest words but by grumbling, sarcasm, arguing, or criticism. Such ungodly reactions of distrust don't magnify our Lord's love even though he demonstrated his love by sending his most precious treasure, his sinless Son, to die on the cross for our salvation.

Apostle Paul tells us to *Do all things without grumbling or disputing* (Philippians 2:14). Shouldn't we know what grumbling means?

Some versions use the word "murmurings" for grumbling. The Greek word for "murmurings" is the same used to describe the Israelites' complaint in the wilderness. The Greek word for "disputing" includes questioning and doubting.

When we grumble we are acknowledging God's plan, but we're saying it's stupid, undesirable, and comes from God's uncaring heart. We are giving him credit but not glory. Surrender comes from being convinced God's plan comes from his heart of love.

Surrender Trusts God's Different Plan

I began this chapter sharing my sin of abuse toward our daughter. I yelled at her constantly and blamed her (and Larry) for all my problems. At different times, I pushed her onto the ground, hit her, and even choked her. I almost used Larry's off-duty service revolver to end my life. When my pleas for an instantaneous deliverance didn't materialize, I believed God's plan wasn't good, and he didn't care about me. Only after I released my plan did he work through his better plan: a process of growth. But, I didn't understand why his ideas would bring him more glory.

A few months ago, I met an elderly woman at a women's retreat. Alice began to tell me about her anxiety. "As you can see, I have a lot of health problems, and I'm a widow without any children. My sister is my caregiver, but it has ruined our relationship. I so desire to have a good relationship with her, but I have to bug her all the time to take care of my medical records, handle my medicines, and take me to doctor appointments. She says I'm nagging her, but I just want her to take good care of me. I'm afraid, and I have no one else."

I could tell Alice was growing more anxious. "I keep asking the Lord to provide another caregiver, but he hasn't. Doesn't he care about me?"

My heart went out to Alice, because she really did need lots of help. *God, why aren't you providing another caregiver?*

Then I saw another possibility. Could God desire a different plan for solving the "problem" by giving Alice and her sister different "hearts"?

I inquired gently, "Alice, maybe he isn't providing another caregiver because he wants you to depend upon him instead of demanding your sister provide what only God can provide, like security?"

I was surprised when tears immediately filled her eyes. "Oh, now I see. I have been angry because it feels like I'm not worthy of care, just like you've talked about in our sessions. I'm trying to force her to make me feel secure. Only God can give security."

I knew this wasn't going to immediately solve all of Alice's difficulties, but it was obvious God was revealing a different perspective to Alice to strengthen her trust in him.

So often, we want to solve our problem or see other people change to create challenge-free, comfortable lives. God is more interested in our character growth and purifying our muddy motives.

Listen to Colleen Fraioli, who is a speaker and author of the Bible study, *Repurposed,* as she shares her own surrender to God's plan.

> I always envisioned making a big splash for God—a perfectly executed dive into the pool of elite speakers and authors. In my head, it looked like a flawless cross between a swan dive and a half gainer, but in fact, my 'splash' looked more like a belly flop.
>
> God pointed out my need for a changed motive through a slew of rejection letters and groveling for editors' attention at writers' conferences. I'd wanted it—recognition, value, admiration— more than I wanted God to be recognized, valued, and admired. Pride definitely cometh before a flop. I finally recognized my need for approval had blocked my calling, and stolen the glory from God. So, in faith I decided to let it die of natural causes.
>
> I noticed a shift in my motives during prayer. I no longer pleaded with God for a better platform, or changing my agent's mind when she decided to let me go. My prayers were more like: 'Father, what do you want to do with this idea? What would be useful for your purposes? Help me write what you want.'
>
> Rather than a stage for my ego, writing has evolved into a place of personal transformation. I'm learning how to swim in his love, for his glory.

Surrender Trusts God's Delayed Plan

I'll never forget walking up to the lectern and greeting the audience as my knees whacked together in my terror. My first ever presentation, and I would be telling my story of how God delivered me from being a child abuser. The audience of young moms was filled with friends from church who had no clue of the monster—me—who sat beside them on Sunday mornings. I never intended to ever tell my story publicly. Oh sure, I'd written an article about God's healing work, but had requested the story be published anonymously.

But through God's obvious orchestration, I obeyed his leading. In the next hour, I shared how God delivered me through a process of growth. I offered solutions for anger I had learned, because he hadn't instantly delivered me. I was shocked to see "light bulbs" of understanding go off in the eyes of many in the audience. Later, several of the young moms approached me saying they were encouraged to know there was hope for them.

When can I do this again?

But no one clamored for me to speak again, except one opportunity at a nearby church.

I was perplexed. *Lord, didn't I glorify you? Where are your open doors for bringing you more glory?*

Looking back now more than thirty-five years later, I can see God's wisdom. My children were young, six and four years old. They needed me available. I could have easily been tempted to become proud with quick "success." I had no real idea of what such a ministry would entail. My marriage still needed lots of attention since we had only just begun to heal. There was so much I didn't know and so much I didn't know I didn't know. God's delay wasn't a "never," it was a "wait."

At times, we think God won't receive glory because his plan is being delayed. But, God is not in a hurry because he knows *his* glory will be revealed—it's just a matter of time, his time. We cooperate with his plan when we surrender to the timing of his will.

God isn't in a hurry because he already knows what's going to happen. You and I are impatient because we want to know his plan. While events unfold and people change slowly, it seems God isn't being glorified.

God isn't in a hurry because he sees our need for sanctification. We finite creatures require time to move through a process of growth. As God's plan develops and we grow stronger in him, he is glorified.

God isn't in a hurry because he sees the end from the beginning. He knows he'll victoriously fulfill his plan for his glory. No need to hurry or worry for him.

We may know someone who turns away from God because God's plan isn't completed in their time line. *He failed me. He doesn't want the best for me after all. How can I trust a God like that?* What motivates such reactions? Here are some possibilities:

- Delay means I'm not important to God. I demand to be valued.

- Delay means insecurity because it's uncertain and confusing. I must figure it out to feel safe.

- Delay slows down my potential success. I must achieve my goals otherwise I'm a failure.

- Delay questions my beliefs about who God is. I've told other people he's going to work in a certain way and now I'll be a liar.

To counteract these lies, we must trust God has a bigger and better plan, even in the midst of delay.

Surrender Doesn't Make Plans for God

The disciples thought they knew Jesus' plan and timing. They often impatiently asked Jesus to fulfill what they thought would bring the most glory to the Father: Israel being delivered from the oppression of the Romans.

So when they had come together, they asked him, 'Lord, will you at this time restore the kingdom to Israel?' He said to them, 'It is not for you to know times or seasons that the Father has fixed by his own authority. But you will receive power when the Holy Spirit has come upon you, and you will be my witnesses in Jerusalem and in all Judea and Samaria, and to the end of the earth.' Acts 1:6-8

Do you hear the passion in their voices? They still think Jesus' main goal is to free Israel from the Romans. Their motives to no longer suffer from their enemies' persecution drove their impatience. Their limited spiritual and mental vision blocked their recognition of God's heart of love through salvation for people.

The above passage occurs after Jesus had risen from the dead and been on earth for forty days. Then the most shocking thing happened. *And while they were gazing into heaven as he went, behold, two men stood by them in white robes, and said, "Men of Galilee, why do you stand looking into heaven? This Jesus, who was taken up from you into heaven, will come in the same way as you saw him go into heaven* (Acts 1:10-11).

Jesus disappears and they stand "gazing." Do they expect him to reappear? Do they anticipate the sudden fulfillment of Israelite rule? We don't know, but it took two angels to bring them out of their "gaze."

God didn't fulfill their plan in their timing. Centuries would pass before Israel would become a nation in 1948. Talk about a delay. But thankfully, they began to understand God's plan and their role in it—spreading the good news of Jesus' life, death, and resurrection.

Sometimes, God's ideas will be different or in a different time frame than we expect. We can surrender as we examine and purify our mixed motives. Jen Wilkin writes about a topic many women struggle with when it comes to God's different ideas: hospitality versus entertaining.

> Entertaining sets the perfect tablescape after an exhaustive search on Pinterest. It chooses a menu that will impress and then frets its way through each stage of preparation. It requires every throw pillow to be in place, every cobweb to be eradicated, every child to be neat and orderly. It plans extra time to don the perfect outfit before the first guest touches the doorbell on the seasonally decorated doorstep. And should any element of the plan fall short, entertaining perceives the entire evening to have been tainted. Entertaining focuses attention on self.

> Hospitality sets a table that makes everyone feel comfortable. It chooses a menu that allows face time with guests instead of being chained to the cooktop. It picks up the house to make things pleasant but doesn't feel the need to conceal evidences of everyday life. It sometimes sits down to dinner with flour in its hair. It allows the gathering to be shaped by the quality of the conversation rather than the cuisine. Hospitality shows interest in the thoughts, feelings, pursuits, and preferences of its guests. It is good at asking questions and listening intently to answers. Hospitality focuses attention on others.

Entertaining is always thinking about the next course. Hospitality burns the rolls because it was listening to a story.
Entertaining obsesses over what went wrong. Hospitality savors what was shared.
Entertaining, exhausted, says, 'It was nothing, really!' Hospitality thinks it was nothing. Really.

Entertaining seeks to impress. Hospitality seeks to bless.
But the two practices can look so similar. Two people can set the same beautiful tablescape and serve the same gourmet meal—one with a motive to impress, the other with a motive to bless. How can we know the difference? Only the second of the two would invite the poor, the crippled, the lame, and the blind to pull up a chair and sip from the stemware. Our motives are revealed not just in how we set our tables but in who we invite to join us at the feast. Entertaining invites those whom it will enjoy. Hospitality takes all comers."[12]

The Disciples
Mark 1:32-38

That evening at sundown they brought to him all who were sick or oppressed by demons. And the whole city was gathered together at the door. And he healed many who were sick with various diseases, and cast out many demons. And he would not permit the demons to speak, because they knew him.

And rising very early in the morning, while it was still dark, he departed and went out to a desolate place, and there he prayed. And Simon and those who were with him searched for him, and they found him and said to him, 'Everyone is looking for you.' And he said to them, 'Let us go on to the next towns, that

I may preach there also, for that is why I came out.' And he went throughout all Galilee, preaching in their synagogues and casting out demons. Mark 1:32-38

Remember, this is very early in this new ministry. The disciples had no clue what they'd gotten into. Jesus had healed numerous people the day before and the whole city was gathered together at the door (vs. 33). What popularity and opportunity.

Knowing the tendencies of people—and their motives—let's use our imagination. After a full day of ministering Jesus heads to bed. Maybe the disciples begin to chat. Impulsive Simon Peter, the visionary, speaks up, "Hey, guys, don't you see what's happening? Jesus' great work will be wonderful for our town. We've already got the whole city on our side. We know there's a plot of land for sale down by the lake and if we start taking an offering, we can gather people together on a regular basis there."

Peter's brother James nods his head. "The Pharisees won't let us meet at the synagogue. They are already mad at Jesus. Let's build a ... what shall we call it?"

The disciples look deep in thought. John's eyes grow big. "Let's call it a ... church."

"Great idea. And if we get big enough, we can call it a ... mega church!"

Then one of the men frowns. "But what if Jesus doesn't want to do this?"

"How could he not?" Simon interjects. "Isn't that why he came, to set up his kingdom? This is how we're finally gonna be freed of those Romans. And we'll give Jesus the corner office with the view of the lake and my office is right next to his. Okay?"

The disciples nod and head to bed. In the morning, they wake up and look into Jesus' bedroom. It's empty. Where is he? There are already sick people at the door and the sun has barely risen. And more people are coming down the road toward the house.

After searching, they finally find him. Simon states, "Jesus! What are you doing? Everyone is looking for you." Is his voice filled with frustration, irritation, or fear?

Then Jesus drops the bombshell. *Let us go on to the next towns, that I may preach there also, for that is why I came out* (vs. 38).

Were the disciples thinking, "Aren't you here to establish your kingdom and defeat the Romans?"

Jesus had tried to make the real plan of bringing glory to God clear to the disciples but their expectations blocked their understanding.

God's plans for his glory may seem delayed or different at times, but be assured God will be glorified. The disciples eventually understood and so can we as we surrender to trusting God knows what he's doing.

Reflection and Discussion Questions

1. When you consider the possibility you might believe you're smarter than God, what do you conclude? If it sometimes seems true, what motivates such a belief?

2. Can you recognize a time when you responded as if you were smarter than God?

3. What did you learn from Job's example? What does God's response to Job (Job 38:1-7) mean to you?

4. Previously, did you see the connection between grumbling and not trusting God? How did you or why didn't you?

5. Can you share an experience when you felt justified to grumble? What happened?

6. What was your reaction to reading, "We are giving him credit but not glory"?

7. When have you felt like Jesus doesn't care? What was the motive behind your grumbling?

8. How do you think seeking God's glory during challenges could empower you to surrender?

9. When God delays his plan, what does that seem to say about how he loves or values you?

10. Describe a time when you really thought you wanted God's glory but you see now you misunderstood God's plan?

11. What is the most important point for you from Jen Wilkin's experience?

12. The disciples were shocked when Jesus had a different plan (Mark 1:32-38). What current expectation might be different from what God wants for you?

Chapter 4

Secure
Know Your Position in Christ

Although salvation is certainly good for man, it is ultimately more about God's glory than man's good. This is why Paul, expounding the great benefits of the gospel in Ephesians, kept repeating that all the blessings of salvation were to the praise of the glory of God's grace (1:6,12, 14)[13].—Michael P.V. Barrett

We all know deep down that we should be perfect. Someone may tell us, 'Now that you believe in Jesus, all your sins are forgiven. There is no condemnation for you. God accepts you.' But simply being told that a few times doesn't solve our problem. We go right back to works-righteousness (that's the natural, default mode of the human heart), and we subjectively stay in bondage to the law even though objectively we are no longer in bondage to it[14].—Timothy Keller

As we chatted, my friend Hannah mentioned, "Kathy, I know we've talked about this before, but I still have a hard time truly believing I'm secure in Christ. I know I became a Christian, and I've become stronger in him, but somehow it just seems scary in some way to think nothing I do can take away my salvation."

Aimee, a Bible college student, talked to me at a retreat and said, "I feel so discouraged when I don't study the Bible every day. I know my salvation isn't in question, but I still feel like I'm not doing enough to represent my security in Christ."

After I asked a few questions, Aimee explained, "I think I need to be filled up spiritually during my quiet time. Then I can resist temptation and glorify God. Shouldn't I be intensely motivated to spend time with God if I say I love him?"

These are the kinds of issues, along with many others, which threaten our sense of security in God's gift of salvation. As a result, our motive can become performing to assure our salvation, rather than resting in who we are in Christ which brings glory to God. But if we are insecure, we are saying he didn't do enough, thus he's incapable and weak.

I say these things not to send us on a guilt trip but to encourage us God wants us to believe we are secure because it's for our benefit and primarily for God's glory.

What Motivates Us?

There can be heart motives driving our inability to trust God for our security. Here are some ideas to ponder.

Security feels like I've lost control. If we feel compelled to be in control, believing God is totally responsible for our salvation can feel like it's out of our hands. *Don't I need to contribute? How can I be sure God will keep his promise if I'm not involved?* Contributing keeps us in control.

Security wasn't taught to me growing up. Because of our upbringing, the message from someone could have been, "Prove your commitment. It's not real unless you live it out completely." Perfectionistic parents or teachers or pastors can easily give the idea we can't be forgiven without paying a kind of "penance." Many women I've spoken to would be ignored for days by a parent because they did something wrong. Such ungodly treatment gives the impression we must earn back love by being good and we transfer such a lie to our relationship with God.

Security indicates I'm weak and needy. To become saved, we recognize our need of a Savior because we are too needy to save ourselves. Once we are saved, we don't want to be needy. If God says he's totally the provider of my security, does that mean I'm inadequate? I don't like thinking of myself that way. I must not be seen as flawed.

These can be deep feelings going back to a wounded childhood. When we are in a vulnerable position being hurt, we decide we'll protect ourselves in the future by standing strong and appearing adequate. Like a threatened porcupine, we grow bigger as if to say, "Get away. I will protect myself." We vow not to be at anyone's mercy again. Depending upon a seemingly untrustworthy God who didn't protect us, feels dangerous again. We're at his mercy. *I'd rather assure my own salvation by working at it or trying to lead a perfect life.*

Hannah, who I mentioned earlier, was sexually abused by her father for many years of her childhood. She felt too unworthy to think God loved her enough to secure her salvation. But over many years, God healed her of the lies the abuse had deposited deep in her heart. And the security of her salvation became real to her.

Aimee grew up in a legalistic church where she constantly heard she could lose her salvation. Her behavior proved whether she really was a Christian. Although our "spiritual fruit" will point to God's Spirit working in us for sanctification, sinning doesn't prove you aren't a Christian or have lost your salvation. The Apostle Paul identified himself as a sinner in his early Epistles. Later, he described himself as a great sinner. Late in life, he called himself the chief of sinners. He became more sensitive to his sin yet he was secure in his salvation—which brought God glory.

If we try to become responsible for our security, we receive glory and steal from God's glory. The Apostle Peter wrote—*to an inheritance that is imperishable, undefiled, and unfading, kept in heaven for you, who by God's power are being guarded through faith for a salvation ready to be revealed in the last time* (I Peter 1:4-5). It's God's power.

Let's look at concepts that can change the lies into truth. God's faithful heart wants you to feel his secure hand upon you.

Fig Leaves Rip

Our sinless, glorious God established the Law of the Old Testament to help us see our need of a coming Messiah and Savior. For some of us, our problem can be thinking we're supposed to keep the Law or perform perfectly to establish and secure our salvation, like my friend Hannah. In a slightly different way, my new Bible student friend, Aimee, also believes her behavior gains favor in God's eyes and even prepares her to obey. Although it's true we need to study the Bible, pray, and other spiritual disciplines, the motive can become warped. We forget abiding in Christ moment by moment empowers us to face life's challenges.

When we depend upon our own performance—even if it's spending time with God—we could be saying, "I find it hard to believe Jesus did enough on the cross for me."

Believing such a lie goes against the truths of Romans 8:2-3. *For the law of the Spirit of life has set you free in Christ Jesus from the law of sin and death. For God has done what the law, weakened by the flesh, could not do. By sending his own Son in the likeness of sinful flesh and for sin, he condemned sin in the flesh.*

We can never fulfill God's holy commandments because our flesh is ... well ... fleshly. It fails us. God designed our flesh to be weak so we would need him.

Curiously, our efforts at performance are exactly what Adam and Eve did after they sinned. To protect themselves from the exposure of their sin's guilt, they hid and designed their own solution—fig leaves. Our fig leaves can be claiming to be perfect, thinking we can reach perfection, or trying to perform as well as possible. All with the motive to override God's plan for our security.

But God knew fig leaves rip and shrivel easily. Instead, he killed animals to provide skins, pointing to the future system of animal sacrifices. And those sacrifices point to the Lamb of God, Jesus, the ultimate sacrifice, who would die in our place on the cross.

When we doubt our security, we're saying his sacrifice wasn't sufficient. That's what I believed as a little girl. I believed God was standing over me, waiting for me to do something wrong so he could punish me. In my child's mind and heart, trying to find a way to protect myself, I envisioned a scale. I piled my good deeds on one side of the scale, my bad deeds on the other. Since nothing could be placed on the "good" side unless done perfectly, I piled the majority of my choices on the "bad" side. My only hope was becoming a perfect adult.

But glory to God, I heard the gospel clearly at the age of eighteen when a boy, Larry (my future and only husband), took me to his church. I understood for the first time nothing I could do would make me good enough to earn God's favor. So God offered salvation to me as a gift through Jesus' death and resurrection. What glorious news! I prayed to receive Christ as my Savior and Lord on Sunday morning, October 1st, 1967. Unfortunately, I thought salvation was also the way for me to act perfectly. It does guarantee perfection in heaven but not on earth. Over these many years, God has been teaching me about grace and how only grace provides security—not what I do.

Can you hear the truth?

You cannot feel guilty enough …

You cannot do enough good deeds …

You cannot mentally hit yourself over the head enough …

You cannot vow to become better to please God …

You can't even have sufficient devotional times to be declared acceptable …

God knew you and I couldn't perform well enough, thus his love designed a plan for declaring us perfect based on Jesus' death and resurrection. God's wrath for sin has been appeased. Satisfied. Taken care of. Perfectly. Completely.

Kris Lundgaard writes, "Your mind can only protect against the deceit of the flesh if you are cross-eyed. That is, you can only keep the rottenness of sin and the kindness of God in mind if you fix your eyes on the cross. What shows God's hatred of sin more than the cross? What shows God's love to you more than the cross? If you want to know exactly what sin deserves, you have to understand the cross. If you want to know how infinitely deep the rot of sin reaches, you have to think through all the implications of the cross. If you want to know how far God was willing to go to rescue you from sin, you have to see his precious Son hanging on the cross for you."[15]

As we learn to rest in such love, God provides other "pointers" to assure us.

The Old Testament Sacrifices Assure Us

It might seem strange to look at the Law, but the Old Testament always points us to Christ. The Bible, including Old and New Testaments, fits together more than we recognize. And the sacrifices beautifully point to Jesus as our sacrifice. Let's look at a particular offering, which speaks to our security. Leviticus 16 gives the procedures for a specific sin and burnt offering involving several bulls and goats. Here's the final step:

> And Aaron shall lay both his hands on the head of the live goat, and confess over it all the iniquities of the people of Israel, and all their transgressions, all their sins. And he shall put them on the head of the goat and send it away into the wilderness by the hand of a man who is in readiness. The goat shall bear all their iniquities on itself to a remote area, and he shall let the goat go free in the wilderness. vss. 21-22

When those verses say a wilderness, they mean no one there. No one will ever see the goat again. It's so far out the goat can't find it's way back. It carries all the sin with it. What a wonderful relief the people must have felt to say "Good bye goat containing my sins forever!"

We have the same relief of saying good bye to our sin because of Jesus, but we're experts at rehearsing our sinful reactions. We say to Jesus, "Remember last month when I yelled at my daughter? I feel so bad. Can I really call myself a Christian?"

What does Jesus say? "Huh? What sin? Well, if you asked me to forgive you, then I've forgiven and forgotten. Why are you rehearsing it when it's not on my radar screen?"

That's security. If Jesus has forgiven and forgotten, our sins are gone and we don't need to feel insecure.

The Torn Curtain Assures Us

At the moment of Jesus' death, Matthew 27:51 tells us, *And behold, the curtain of the temple was torn in two, from top to bottom.* By God's original design the sanctuary was composed of three parts. First, the Outer Court where anyone was allowed—even Gentiles. Secondly, the Holy Place where any priest entered as they burned incense and trimmed the lamps. Finally, the Holy of Holies where the High Priest could only enter once a year on the Day of Atonement. Before he entered that sacred place, he went through an elaborate ceremony of becoming totally cleansed from all sin. If he wasn't completely cleansed, God had indicated he would be quickly killed inside the Holy of Holies. The temple's design pointed to God's holiness.

Before Jesus died, he had said, *Do not think that I have come to abolish the Law or the Prophets; I have not come to abolish them but to fulfill them* (Matthew 5:17). At the moment of Jesus' death, he fulfilled the law. The curtain was torn from top to bottom assuring us God himself had made the Holy of Holies available to us. If a person had torn the curtain, he would have ripped it from bottom to top. Only God could start at the top because it was very big.

The destruction of the curtain was a physical representation for the Jews and Gentiles. Today it is a symbolic representation convincing us it is God's work of providing salvation, not us "working" or "being good enough." Jesus fulfilled all the requirements of the Law we aren't able to keep. There is no "curtain" separating us from having a relationship with a holy God. When we think we need to be perfect or do anything sufficiently, we are re-hanging the veil. God hasn't put it back up. Let's not put it back either—it's too heavy.

Christ's Resurrection Assures You

We often focus on the beautiful gift of salvation through Christ's death and forget the importance of his resurrection. In I Corinthians 15:3-4, the Apostle Paul stresses both: *For I delivered to you as of first importance what I also received: that Christ died for our sins in accordance with the Scriptures, that he was buried, that he was raised on the third day in accordance with the Scriptures.*

Jesus is no longer in the grave! Jesus' resurrection verified him as the true Messiah. Many men died on crosses and some may have claimed to be the long-awaited Messiah, but none of them rose from the grave. Without the resurrection, Jesus death as evidence of his Messiahship is suspect. But the resurrection confirmed Jesus' words: "It is finished." The empty grave declares God saying, "See? It really is true! Jesus was no imposter. This is my stamp of approval. I'm satisfied with my Son's death on the cross in your place to wipe away all your sin. Therefore, you can live in confidence." Romans 4:5 affirms, *And to the one who does not work but believes in him who justifies the ungodly, his faith is counted as righteousness.* Do you notice "who does not work"? Working for our salvation or to keep our salvation is not needed.

No wonder Satan loves to attack our security. When we are wondering whether enough has been done we become nervous. When someone "sees us" as imperfect, we wonder if they are questioning our salvation. Our lack of confidence motivates our defensiveness and anger.

When we counteract Satan's questioning whispers with the truth, we live confidently. The Apostle Paul reminds us, *and what is the immeasurable greatness of his power toward us who believe, according to the working of his great might that he worked in Christ when he raised him from the dead and seated him at his right hand in the heavenly places* (Ephesians 1:19-20).

The same resurrection power is available to you and me. We won't use it perfectly, but we'll grow stronger, which is the process of sanctification. Additionally, because he's no longer in the grave, Jesus is at the right hand of the Father, interceding for us. No wonder we can be assured of our salvation.

Our High Priest Assures Us

Because Jesus is interceding for us before the Father's throne, we have someone claiming us as his own. He declares, "This is my beloved daughter, and see? Our Spirit resides in her guaranteeing her salvation."

The writer of Hebrews tells us the significance of this.

He is able to save to the uttermost those who draw near to God through him, since he always lives to make intercession for them. For it was indeed fitting that we should have such a high priest, holy, innocent, unstained, separated from sinners, and exalted above the heavens. He has no need, like those high priests, to offer sacrifices daily, first for his own sins and then for those of the people, since he did this once for all when he offered up himself. For the law appoints men in their weakness as high priests, but the word of the oath, which came later than the law, appoints a Son who has been made perfect forever. Hebrews 7:25-28

Those verses contrast the work of Jewish priests making sacrifices over and over again with Jesus' death, once. The difference is Jesus died once and took care of the sacrifice forever. Nothing else needs to be done. But Satan's evil, condemning whispers haunt us saying the opposite. Satan is even audacious enough to accuse us before God's throne (Revelation 12:10). But Jesus defends us and proclaims we are secure in our salvation because he purchased it.

God knew we could never do it right "enough," so he provided a plan which not only benefits us but brings him glory. It's all about him. We have nothing to offer. And when we see how great our salvation is at Jesus' expense, we are filled with gratitude which prompts our willing obedience thus magnifying his gracious love and power.

Our Inheritance in Christ Assures Us

Looking to the Old Testament for descriptions of our inheritance in Christ may seem strange, but remember, before Jesus ever came, God was pointing to his coming and what it would mean for believers. Zechariah 3:1-5 is helpful for this.

> Then he showed me Joshua the high priest standing before the angel of the Lord [Jesus], and Satan standing at his right hand to accuse him. And the Lord said to Satan, "The Lord rebuke you, O Satan! The Lord who has chosen Jerusalem rebuke you! Is not this a brand plucked from the fire?" Now Joshua was standing before the angel, clothed with filthy garments. And the angel said to those who were standing before him, "Remove the filthy garments from him." And to him he said, "Behold, I have taken your iniquity away from you, and I will clothe you with pure vestments." And I said, "Let them put a clean turban on his head." So they put a clean turban on his head and clothed him with garments. And the angel of the Lord was standing by.

Joshua as the High Priest represents God's people before the "angel of the Lord," which is another name for Jesus. "Brand" refers to a converted soul. The Lord is replying, "Yes, you're right, Satan. Joshua and all people deserve fire but I have chosen to pull them out and it will be a testimony of my greatness."

No wonder Satan is fighting hard. He just can't stand God being glorified. He hates God and to battle God, he attacks those God loves. Satan accuses us, "See how you act? You aren't really saved. God is holy and he must give up on you."

Or Satan whispers, "Oh sure, you're saved but you better put in the time for study and prayer. Otherwise, you won't have the power you need to resist temptation."

Without God's gracious gift of salvation and empowering Holy Spirit, both are true. But verse 4 provides the solution—resulting in his glory. Jesus, the angel of the Lord, says, "remove those filthy rags." Even though at the time of Zechariah Jesus hasn't died on the cross nor risen from the grave, God already has designed the plan. Salvation isn't a last minute, stop gap measure. God didn't become so disgusted with our sin that he said, "Well, they just can't seem to get their act together no matter how much they try. I guess I'll have to take care of them, poor little weak things."

We must see the plan of salvation as designed by God before he even formed the earth. He knew his first creatures with his image would sin. He provided animal skins pointing to salvation through Jesus' sacrifice and resurrection. This is great news! And here in Zechariah, God is already pointing to our inheritance in Christ.

God deserves the glory because he provides the only solution: Joshua's filthy rags are removed. Joshua represents not only the people of Israel but us as well. Our iniquity is removed and we are clothed with pure vestments. We receive a clean turban and pure, magnificent garments, which speak of God's provision and love.

I can understand if you're still a little dubious about how all this can refer to Jesus, but a few verses later, verse 8 gives us the key. *Hear now, O Joshua the high priest, you and your friends who sit before you, for they are men who are a sign: behold, I will bring my servant the Branch.*

Who is this servant, the Branch? It's another name for Jesus and his coming work of redemption. Numerous verses refer to the coming Messiah as the Branch or variations of the Hebrew word "shoot": Isaiah 4:2, 11:1, 53:2; Jeremiah 33:15; Ezekiel 17:22-24, 34:29.

So what is our turban and new garments? The Bible is filled with descriptions of them. The first chapter of Ephesians is most likely the most extensive listing. Take a look:

vs. 3: every spiritual blessing
vs. 4: chosen, holy, blameless, loved
vs. 5: predestined, adopted
vs. 6: grace freely bestowed
vs. 7: redeemed, forgiven, given rich grace
vs. 8: lavish grace
vs. 9: enlightened understanding
vs. 11: inheritance, fulfillment of his purposes
vs. 12: ability to give God praise
vs. 13: sealed by Holy Spirit
vs. 14: Holy Spirit in us as a pledge of our inheritance
vs. 17: wisdom, revelation to know Christ
vs. 18: enlightened eyes
vs. 22: part of church body
vs. 23: spiritual body of Christ.

I would really encourage you to meditate on those blessings at length.

Our Adoption Assures Us

Let's concentrate on how Ephesians 1:5 can speak to us to give us a deeper sense of security: *he predestined us for adoption as sons through Jesus Christ, according to the purpose of his will.* Interestingly, in the Roman culture when Paul wrote this Epistle, a Roman father could disinherit a son born into the family. But an adopted child could not be disinherited. The idea was a father had no choice as to what he received when a baby was born naturally into the family. If the child grew up and disgraced the family, the father could justify disinheriting him by saying, "I didn't know he had all these flaws, otherwise I wouldn't have chosen him."

But an adopted child was chosen specifically with full knowledge of his strengths, weaknesses, appearance, and anything else a family considered important. Therefore, a father could not justify disinheriting him. A father could never say, "I didn't know what I was getting."

Paul's wording didn't just say we are sons (or daughters). He included the fact we are adopted. Paul fully knew the Roman culture—he was Jewish yet had Roman citizenship. His readers knew the significance of not only becoming a son but an adopted son—a position which could not be taken away regardless of performance or flaws.

I hope this speaks to you as much as it speaks to me. God wants us to know we cannot be disinherited—we cannot lose our salvation! He chose us fully knowing we would not be perfect. But he also wants us to desire to please him out of gratitude for the great salvation he has given us. As we live in that assurance, we'll give glory to God.

When you read through Ephesians 1, it's striking how often God's glory is mentioned. You'll find it in:

vs. 6: his grace brings him glory

vs. 12: we are to the praise of his glory

vs. 14: the gift of the Holy Spirit brings praise to his glory

vs. 17: God is the Father of glory

vs. 18: we can know the riches of his glory revealed in our inheritance.

What glorious connections to our inheritance.

If you are a Christian, you are secure. You may not always "feel" it, but you are regardless of your feelings. As we more fully develop joy and a sense of security we enlarge God's generosity in the eyes of others.

I recently talked again with my friend Hannah. It had been a while since we'd addressed her insecurity about her salvation. When I brought it up, I was amazed with her reaction.

With almost a vehemence, she declared, "Oh, Kathy, I don't believe that any more. I know for sure I'm saved and going to heaven. Nothing is going to take that away."

I giggled with delight hearing of such confidence. It had been a long journey for her. What a relief to know she has confidence in God's work in her. I know her family and friends notice it.

The Rich Young Ruler
Mark 10:17-22

And as he was setting out on his journey, a man ran up and knelt before him and asked him, "Good Teacher, what must I do to inherit eternal life?" And Jesus said to him, "Why do you call me good? No one is good except God alone. You know the commandments: 'Do not murder, Do not commit adultery, Do not steal, Do not bear false witness, Do not defraud, Honor your father and mother.'" And he said to him, "Teacher, all these I have kept from my youth." And Jesus, looking at him, loved him, and said to him, "You lack one thing: go, sell all that you have and give to the poor, and you will have treasure in heaven; and come, follow me." Disheartened by the saying, he went away sorrowful, for he had great possessions. Mark 10:17-22

The rich young ruler considered himself faultless over his whole life. Who really does that?

Any of us who think we can earn a secure salvation is putting a huge burden upon ourselves, which God never intended us to carry. In fact—hold onto your seats—it steals God's glory. This young man gets the glory. The Law points to our need for redemption and salvation because we can't do it ourselves. The rich young ruler didn't believe that.

Jesus calls him out. "Are you saying I'm God? Only God is good so therefore you must be calling me God. Is that true?" Jesus is the expert "asker" to draw out our motives—and a call for action. In this case, this "ruler" secretly values his possessions, which block his willingness to surrender to Jesus. His heart is "double-motivated." He mentions what he feels comfortable in revealing—his perfection. His passion is not to bring glory to God but to have everyone shine his sparkling halo.

I love Jesus' response: *And Jesus, looking at him, loved him, and said to him ...* (vs. 21).

Wouldn't you love to actually see Jesus' "look"? We can only imagine the sorrow mixed with deep love. Jesus wants the best for him and will risk rejection to tell him the truth. In my paraphrase, Jesus says, "Sell all your possessions and give to the poor because then you are truly worshipping. Admit your needy heart and then follow me. Your commitment to perform perfectly *will* fail. But I offer you acceptance and life despite your imperfections—which you have conveniently ignored."

The young man turned and walked away.

You don't have to be insecure like this young man. Jesus looks at you with love, wanting you to have the assurance of knowing he has done everything needed to secure you as God's chosen daughter, a princess.

Reflection and Discussion Questions

1. What do you think about Michael Barrett's quote: "Although salvation is certainly good for man, it is ultimately more about God's glory ..."?

2. To what degree do you feel secure in your salvation? Can you identify any beliefs contributing to a lack of assurance?

3. If you've never confessed being a sinner and receiving Christ as your Lord and Savior, what would you like to do about that?

4. If you sometimes feel like you're not doing "enough," what might help you to focus on the "enough" of what Christ has done?

5. Was there anything from the Old Testament goat sacrifice meaningful to you?

6. How does the torn curtain speak to you?

7. Had you considered how Christ's resurrection pointed to your security? If so, in what way? Did you discover anything new from this section?

8. How does having Jesus as your High Priest assure you of your salvation? Does that motivate you to bring more glory to God? In what way?

9. What is most meaningful to you about the Zechariah 3:1-5 passage?

10. Which of the element(s) of your inheritance from Ephesians 1 is most meaningful to you and why?

11. How does the Roman law of not disinheriting adopted children speak to you?

12. Which part of the Rich Young Ruler story is most important to you and a sense of your security?

13. How do you want being secure in your salvation to purify your motives to give greater glory to God?

Chapter 5

Satisfied
Enjoy Contentment

Perfectionism seeks to remove any possibility of criticism from every aspect of performance.[16]—Heather Davis Nelson

The true Christian ideal is not to be happy but to be holy.[17]—A.W. Tozer

As I was talking with a women's ministry director at a church training conference, I hoped she would invite me to speak at her women's retreat. I enjoyed one of the freshly baked chocolate chip cookies set before us while we sat in the lounge of the convention center. When she asked my opinion on some important issues, I spoke with confident tones. I was thrilled to see her staring at my mouth, obviously eager to hear my every word. Surely, I was impressing her. *All I have to do is say the right things*, I assured myself, as I anxiously tried to think of what those "right things" might be.

After we concluded, I headed for the restroom feeling content with the open door God had given me. I walked through the restroom door and saw my reflection in the mirror. *What's that dark thing on my lip?* I went closer and realized chocolate was dripping down my lip and chin. *Oh, no, how long has that been there?* I realized the mess had decorated my face during most of our conversation. For whatever reason, she had not felt comfortable telling me.

Oh, Lord, what have you done to me? What about my pithy statements and wise admonitions? How foolish I must have looked. How humiliating!

In a flash of truth, I recognized my dissatisfaction with God's plan. And I started laughing. *Oh, Lord, you do have a sense of humor. Please forgive me for my pride and self-importance. I fell into that trap again.* But I also acknowledged God's power because rather than being discontent with myself for the next five days (like other times), the reflection in the bathroom mirror brought immediate joy.

It's a challenge to trust God and give him glory in a culture of striving, competition, people pleasing, entitlement, regrets, and so many other perspectives which reap discontent. Contentment is wiped out by keeping up with the Jones'. Television commercials labor to convince us our laundry detergent needs to smell good or else we're not doing a good job. Climb the ladder of success and you'll feel satisfied. Discover your inner muse and be emotionally healthy. Wear the latest designer clothes. Find the diet which will finally work for you—forever—otherwise you'll never feel content with your body. The list is endless and each promise is striving to create discontentment so we'll buy the latest product or join the latest group.

Mixed motives can block us from godly satisfaction in many areas but in this chapter we'll only be able to concentrate on five: people pleasing, pride, comparisons, perfectionism, and performance.

People Pleasing

Jan Johnson, popular speaker and author of *Abundant Simplicity* and many other books, worked on study guides for books by Dallas Willard. She wrote in her newsletter:

> After one of his [Dallas Willard] talks, I was thanking him for writing *The Spirit of the Disciplines*. In my earnestness to be authentic, I spoke of not trying to ingratiate myself to him. Then he made a ridiculous suggestion, saying, 'Why don't you try not affirming anyone for a while, and see what happens?' I knew this had to be wrong because encouraging people is a good thing, so I dismissed the suggestion.
>
> But as time passed, I found that each time I started to encourage someone, I listened to my motives, wondering: Is God leading me to do this? Or am I trying to get people to like me? Or look up to me? Sometimes I was truly selfless, but other times (ugh!) I secretly wanted to be loved and admired. Dallas's suggestion became one of many steps that helped me move away from impression management.[18]

I love Jan's wording: "impression management," which defines people pleasing exactly. Our eyes are on other's opinions rather than God's. Proverbs 29:25 warns us, *The fear of man lays a snare, but whoever trusts in the Lord is safe.*

We won't be surprised to learn Jesus's disciples had similar "impression management" challenges. In Matthew 15, Jesus has a discussion with the Pharisees and they are unhappy. The disciples say to Jesus, *Do you know that the Pharisees were offended when they heard this [your] saying?"* (vs. 12).

The disciples must have expected Jesus to exclaim, "Oh, no. Really? I didn't expect my words would offend them. I'll go immediately and ask their forgiveness. I'll be more careful next time."

Not quite. Jesus doesn't change the Father's plan or diminish speaking the truth because those "in power" are upset. If he did, he would have been motivated by discontent with the lack of acceptance by others. As we talked about in our first chapter on loving others well, he would actually be loving the Pharisees *poorly* by encouraging them to continue in their false beliefs and sin. He loved them *well* by challenging them and correcting them.

They didn't receive his correction, but Jesus didn't feel responsible to force them to change. Neither was Jesus discontent as if they empowered his ministry's success. Jesus didn't have a single people-pleasing bone in his body.

Let me ask you—and myself. Who do we believe

- opens ministry doors?
- brings a promotion?
- delivers our child from drugs?
- prompts our husband/friend/boss to listen to us?
- brings healing?

Only God holds the key to everything he wants for us. He only plans and intends what will bring him the exaltation he deserves. We can diminish people pleasing by keeping our eyes on him. Especially to our family members and friends ruled by "impression management," we will represent a contentment fueled by confidence in God's sovereign goodness which provides everything we need.

Pride

The satisfaction-stealer pride can be difficult to identify. It can be so subtle it's tentacles seem invisible. Like an attacked octopus, it ejects ink into the water to ensure its safety. Pride hides behind a self-satisfaction refusing to see weakness or lies. Interestingly, pride is often the result of a heart lacking confidence in self. To examine our hearts is terrifying because our high-rise strategy might tumble down and expose us in the way we don't want to be seen.

Pride can be seen in the strategy of entitlement. I'm guilty. As I drive my car, pride thinks everyone should make me the priority. If someone cuts me off my heart thinks they did it on purpose. *Don't you know how important I am? Don't you dare suggest I'm stupid or not valuable by the way you treat me.*

Bethany Jenkins, Director of The Gospel Coalition's Every Square Inch, experienced a similar kind of challenge in the grocery store. She writes,

> On Sunday afternoon, in the checkout line at the grocery store, I put a man on trial. He made no argument and offered no defense, but I judged him guilty.
>
> I went there to pick up three things—fruit, deli meat, and club soda. When I got to the only open line, there was just one man ahead of me. *This is going to be quick,* I assumed.
>
> After the cashier started ringing up his items, though, he decided it was a good time to ask where the pre-made guacamole was. "Aisle 5," she said. Then he left his place in line to find it.
>
> When he returned a few minutes later, the cashier had finished scanning his items and customers had started lining up, but his hands were empty. He hadn't found the guacamole. "It's on aisle 7," another store employee said. "On the bottom shelf." The man again went to search.
>
> Five minutes later, with eight customers now in line, he finally checked out. And I was annoyed. *Why did he wait and ask the cashier? Why didn't he ask someone else before he got in line? How could he inconvenience the rest of us like this?* The only reasonable answer, I concluded, was he was rude, incompetent, and narcissistic.
>
> As I walked home, though, I wondered why my heart went so easily to judgment and anger, not to grace and mercy. *Why did*

I spend so much time mentally logging the reasons he was guilty, not the reasons he might need grace? Why did my time need so much defending?

How little I knew of this stranger, yet how easily I judged him based on a single 10-minute interaction—and we didn't even exchange a word.

Proud hearts are always unhappy and complaining about situations and people. They think they know the way their lives should go and how others should behave—and how quickly they should be able to check out at the grocery store.

Humble hearts, though, search Scripture and let Scripture search them. They receive from others and from God. They're flexible, not controlling. They think, *Things are messy right now, but who knows? Maybe I need this. I know God must have a reason for it. I guess you know best, Lord.*[19]

I appreciate Bethany's vulnerable sharing. She has identified the key to contentment: giving God glory and "the benefit of the doubt" about what his loving motives are for allowing challenging circumstances.

Strangely, pride and people pleasing are related. People pleasing is motivated by my need to be seen as valued, and pride is motivated by my demand to be seen as important. Only allowing God to humble us and then recognizing we all are equally sinful and insufficient at the foot of the cross will bring godly contentment thus pointing to the magnificence of God.

Comparisons

Have you ever found yourself thinking, "I'll make sure I'm never bad like her." Or "I want to be good like her." We all have and it may seem like a really good thing to focus on avoiding the mistakes of some and emulating the good points of others. Even the Apostle Paul wrote to his friends in Philippi, *Brothers, join in imitating me, and keep your eyes on those who walk according to the example you have in us* (3:17).

But if we read his words earlier in that chapter, he says, *Not that I have already obtained this or am already perfect, but I press on to make it my own, because Christ Jesus has made me his own. Brothers, I do not consider that I have made it my own. But one thing I do: forgetting what lies behind and straining forward to what lies ahead, I press on toward the goal for the prize of the upward call of God in Christ Jesus* (Philippians 3:12-14).

Paul isn't saying "be like me" so much as he's saying be like how I'm like Jesus. Paul acknowledges he is imperfect and still on a spiritual journey himself.

When we point others to be like Jesus as we are learning to be like Jesus (to whatever extent) we are lifting up the greatness of Christ. We are never supposed to idolize a friend as the example, only how they reflect Christ.

Other people will always fail us. To put our satisfaction in being like them is surely like building our house on sand ... near the waves ... as a hurricane approaches. A very saddening comment I hear is, "Well, my pastor failed me and now I don't go to church." Such an attitude reveals they put their focus on someone who was never meant to be their example. When we are disappointed by others, our objective wasn't to be like Jesus.

Of course, there's nothing wrong with gaining wisdom from another believer or noticing characteristics in them you need to improve in. But what is our motive? If we think being like them will give us the contentment we need, we aren't acknowledging our perfect model Jesus as our source of goodness. We want to give others a correct opinion about who Jesus is, not another Christian.

Perfectionism

Since I write and speak on perfectionism so often, many women have told me, "Oh, I know I'm not a perfectionist. My house is a mess and I never do anything perfect." They define perfectionism incorrectly. The perfectionist never reaches perfection. She believes she can't be satisfied until she achieves it. She also believes God is expecting her to become perfect and he's dissatisfied with her until she does.

Because so many women (and men) find it difficult to identify any perfectionistic tendencies in themselves (even though many around them can), I developed a quiz to help. Here it is. Keep track of which statements apply to you, even if it's not applicable to your life all the time.

1. _____I keep waiting to become better so that God can love me completely.
2. _____I spend lots of energy evaluating my performance.
3. _____I tend to think in terms of "all or nothing."
4. _____I think I should have my act together by now.
5. _____My expectations tend to be unrealistic.
6. _____For me, "good" is rarely "good enough."
7. _____I often wonder why people can't get their act together.
8. _____I'm compelled to straighten out misunderstandings.
9. _____I won't begin something if there's a possibility I can't do it well. [20]

Add up the number of statements you relate to. If you scored three or more of those statements, you have perfectionistic tendencies.

When I give this quiz at speaking engagements, women are shocked to see how they can apply those characteristics to themselves more than they realize. They are surprised to learn even four statements indicates perfectionistic thinking. Many say, "I thought I needed to identify with all nine statements to be a perfectionistic." It doesn't work like that. Even a person with one characteristic could be dissatisfied with her life because she's waiting to no longer succumb to that characteristic.

Perfectionism is often developed because of painful experiences in our early years. When hurtful things happen, as children with limited understanding, we aren't able to figure out the cause. Children blame themselves. We might think, "If I can just be better, even perfect, I'll deserve good treatment. If I'm good, I'll protect myself from pain."

As one example, I've heard numerous stories where women decided when their parents divorced it must have been their fault because "I didn't get A's on my report card" or "I failed to obey." The conclusion wasn't mommy or daddy made unwise choices, but "I must have done something wrong." As a result, that child decides to prevent further difficulties by doing everything right.

There are any number of causes of perfectionism, including sexual abuse. But they usually stem from trying to make a broken world right by making themselves behave. Even if the child becomes a Christian, the self-protective strategy is already in place and God patiently begins to chip away at it.

My own story of developing perfectionism had those elements. Even though I've now been a Christian almost fifty years, I'm still in process of developing greater trust in God motivated by desiring God's glory. I learn again and again God doesn't expect me to be perfect on this earth—and the same applies to you.

Paul's very words prove that. Remember his words?

Not that I have already obtained this or am already perfect, but I press on to make it my own, because Christ Jesus has made me his own. Brothers, I do not consider that I have made it my own. But one thing I do: forgetting what lies behind and straining forward to what lies ahead, I press on toward the goal for the prize of the upward call of God in Christ Jesus. Philippians 3:12-14

Most people consider Paul's letter to the Philippians the book of joy and contentment. Included in his encouragement, he wrote about his own imperfections and God's realistic expectations of his earthly children.

Paul emphasized:

- We'll never become perfect on this earth. We'll always be "in process." *And I am sure of this, that he who began a good work in you will bring it to completion at the day of Jesus Christ* (1:6).

- Seek excellence not perfection. Excellence is doing the best we can with what we already have learned. It means knowing there will always be more we can learn. Perfection means never sinning and is unattainable. *And it is my prayer that your love may abound more and more, with knowledge and all discernment, so that you may approve what is excellent, and so be pure and blameless for the day of Christ,* (vss. 9-10).

- After we become a Christian, we'll be dependent upon God's continuing work. *Therefore, my beloved, as you have always obeyed, so now, not only as in my presence but much more in my absence, work out your own salvation with fear and trembling, for it is God who works in you, both to will and to work for his good pleasure* (2:12-13).

- Continue to learn. God uses our circumstances to develop more contentment. *I know how to be brought low, and I know how to abound. In any and every circumstance, I have learned the secret of facing plenty and hunger, abundance and need* (4:9).

In addition, to the Corinthians he writes, *And we all, with unveiled face, beholding the glory of the Lord, are being transformed into the same image from one degree of glory to another* (2 Corinthians 3:18). Seeing God's glory assists the transformation of our growth in glory (our godliness) even on this earth.

I hope this is encouraging. Don't let perfectionism diminish or destroy growth in being satisfied in God's good gifts. Have confidence and satisfaction that God loves us enough he'll never give up on us nor stop investing in our lives.

Performance

As humans, we are creative in finding ungodly ways to strive for what God wants to give us freely. He designs godly ways for us to give him glory but our fears put obstacles in his way. One of those is judging our worth and value by our performance. The world, especially the American culture, screams it's messages "be productive," "look good," "appear all together," and so many others. Yet God's way is different: rest in him and find your contentment in him.

One area we Christian women often strive to "look good" is hospitality. We so encumber ourselves with the perfect dessert recipe or magnificent centerpiece, we often miss an opportunity to reveal God's own gracious hospitality who welcomes all and does not require perfection to enjoy his fellowship. Sadly, we drive ourselves crazy—which doesn't glorify God—while thinking we are exalting God with our show of being all together. *That's* craziness, not contentment.

Or we fill up our calendars thinking God looks good. Yet we are impatient, frustrated, and graceless. We complain we don't have time to study the Bible, yet we can give the latest information from the style magazine we poured over. We are worried our child's disobedience speaks ill of God's work in our lives, yet we neglect reading a parenting book because our commitments at church leave little time for reading.

Please don't misunderstand. I'm guilty of all these things and more. Until we stop and question our motives, we'll be less attentive to see God's invitation to give us a pure heart.

So let's ask ourselves,

- Am I taking on this project for the Mother's Day tea because I want God's glory or because I can't say no. If I say no, I might give the impression I can't do everything and anything.

- Am I joining this committee because I've seen how disorganized the leader is and they need me to straighten it out?

- Am I signing up to take a meal to the new mom on a

day already filled to the brim because saying no will make her feel like I don't care or love her? Or version two: The group is using an online sign-up program. Wonder if everyone notices I haven't signed up?

- Do I feel compelled to 'like' this post on Facebook or pass along the next online "chain letter" because otherwise my friend won't think I'm supporting her?

- Am I feeling disgruntled because I'm not having a lot of responses on my Facebook or Twitter post?

- Am I working hard on the church event so everyone will see how creative I am, rather than looking to God for his approval and applause?

Of course, in all these things, we will have mixed motives. We do want God's glory and yet Satan craftily sneaks in thoughts of selfishness and self-aggrandizement. God's desire is to purify us to a greater extent, not perfectly, but desiring him exalted regardless of what we gain. And in the process he will create within us satisfaction and contentment.

My friend and author Lynn Morrissey's story hits home.

I didn't say it to him, because he was my boss and a pastor. I didn't raise my voice and I remained seated, but mentally, I was on my feet and my emotions were rising precipitously. *You want me to do what?* I questioned silently … with exasperation and, admittedly, a bit of resentment.

As he continued to describe my role opening each morning's VBS session, I still couldn't believe it. He wanted me (*me!*) to portray a pink hippopotamus named Miss Hippo as I encouraged the kids in a fun romp through the Bible. My attitude would be key in setting the tone for each morning of learning about the Bible.

But a pink hippopotamus?

Good grief! I was the church's respected Director of Christian Education, and formerly the Executive Director of the world's largest airport USO. It had been hard to leave that full-time career at forty to raise our daughter. I missed the personal accolades and professional camaraderie. I had taken the part-time church job and in my arrogance considered it a step-down. Now God was permitting my utter humiliation in playing a Pepto-Bismol pink mammoth mammal in front of a multitude of children and their teachers. It was embarrassing. I almost refused.

But the Holy Spirit instantly reminded me he can be glorified when I am mortified. God had taught me many painful lessons about my pride in the past. But God also showed me time and again, how mortification, in its truest sense, doesn't involve shame and degradation. Mortification means 'putting to death.' The Lord was asking me to die to myself, to my selfish aspirations for the sake of others, because he had something special in mind.

Though reluctantly, I humbled myself before God and never complained to the pastor. I donned a perky pink wig and adopted a high-pitched hippo voice, like Miss Piggy on steroids. And for the next two weeks I hippo high-fived my way down the center aisle of the church, slapping hands with eager kids and shouting a friendly hippo-hello on my way to the pulpit. And each morning, I watched the children's wide-eyed wonder as Miss Hippo shared exciting Bible passages, bringing ancient stories and characters to life. The kids grew more excited by the day, and I grew more humbled. God brought a number of children to himself that summer. When I died to 'Lynn' and served his children, God got all the glory.

The Seventy-Two
Luke 10

I'm sure the disciples were excited, yet tense, when Jesus told them his next assignment for them. *After this the Lord appointed seventy-two others and sent them on ahead of him, two by two, into every town and place where he himself was about to go* (Luke 10:1).

Although we don't know all that happened on their little excursion, they returned triumphant telling Jesus joyfully about all the work they had done for him. *The seventy-two returned with joy, saying, "Lord, even the demons are subject to us in your name!"* (vs. 17).

Can't you just picture the broad smile on Jesus's face as he exclaimed, "You all are amazing and should be very proud of yourselves for your cooperation with your Heavenly Father. What a sense of satisfaction you must feel seeing the Spirit empower you. I'm so impressed. I want you to be assured God has been glorified by all you did. Rejoice because many souls were brought into the kingdom. You did well!"

Hmmmm. Well, not really. Listen to Jesus's reply.

And he said to them, "I saw Satan fall like lightning from heaven. Behold, I have given you authority to tread on serpents and scorpions, and over all the power of the enemy, and nothing shall hurt you. Nevertheless, do not rejoice in this, that the spirits are subject to you, but rejoice that your names are written in heaven." vss. 18-20

I didn't travel with those followers but if I had, and heard Jesus's words, I would have been upset. *What? Are you kidding, Jesus? I did great things for you and you're treating it like nothing. After all the trekking, and the rejection by many, you're telling me I shouldn't find satisfaction from all I accomplished? My focus should be in knowing I'm going to heaven? But if I understand your message right, I didn't do anything to deserve that. You are going to do it all. What kind of satisfaction do I get from that?*

Exactly!

Of course, they don't yet know about Jesus's coming crucifixion and resurrection, which is what their salvation will be based upon. You and I know that but at this point, the seventy-two believe spreading the good news about Jesus and setting people free is what brings satisfaction.

That's not Jesus's perspective for glorifying God. It's not production or performance. It's their destination of heaven signifying the glory of the Father's provision of salvation through Jesus's death and resurrection—to his credit.

Let's learn the lesson the seventy-two did. Although God intends to use us, our satisfaction comes from seeing him magnified in the eyes of others, not reveling in our efforts.

Reflection and Discussion Questions

1. Can you think of an example when God gave you an opportunity to examine the mixed motives behind your satisfaction in earthly things?

2. How do you think you are most influenced toward dissatisfaction by your culture's belief system?

3. Do you consider yourself a people pleaser? Explain your yes or no. If you are, give one example.

4. What seems to be threatened within you if you don't please everyone? What might the Lord want you to sacrifice to purify your motives?

5. To what degree do you think you struggle with pride? Explain.

6. What is one way you see pride exhibited in your life?

7. Can you give one example of entitlement in your life? What were you hoping for by getting what you thought you deserved?

8. Can you share a time when you were impacted by a Christian not living up to your expectations? What happened?

9. What was your score on the perfectionist quiz and how did you react?

10. What did you learn about yourself from the quiz?

11. Which of the verse(s) by Paul about God's attitude toward your growth means the most to you?

12. When performing takes your focus off of God, what do you hope to gain?

13. What was important to you in the passage about the "Seventy-Two"?

Chapter 6

Stable
Reap Emotional Strength

When God disappoints our idolatrous desires, we can offer profound gratitude for his jealousy. Not getting what we want can be salvation indeed.[21]—Jen Pollock Michel

Can you see how awesome it is to know that you have been created for God's glory? That you are to live in such a way as to give all of creation a correct opinion or estimate of who God is?[22]—Kay Arthur

My friend Christina described what had occurred the day before. "My four-year-old jumped in the deep side of the swimming pool and struggled with keeping his head above the water. He ended up swallowing some water and coughed a bit after. Apart from the little scare, he was fine. But my worrying mind played tricks on me, and I kept thinking about one thing—delayed drowning. They say it's very rare but what if it would happen to my son? So, of course I researched it and read like ten different articles. Crazy, but also human. I fought with myself and ended up tossing my phone on the couch, closing my eyes, and asking the Lord to forgive me for worrying and to protect my son from any form of drowning. So, Kathy, maybe I worry too much at times but I know whom I can turn to and I feel so very blessed."

I appreciated Christina's frank sharing. Of course, I could relate. I struggle to keep my head above water trusting God and allowing him to rule my emotions. I know my emotional stability will bring glory to God because emotional strength is the opposite of what the world experiences. Yet, so often I feel like the man the Apostle James describes:

> If any of you lacks wisdom, let him ask God, who gives generously to all without reproach, and it will be given him. But let him ask in faith, with no doubting, for the one who doubts is like a wave of the sea that is driven and tossed by the wind. For that person must not suppose that he will receive anything from the Lord; he is a double-minded man, unstable in all his ways. James 1:5-8

Too often, my heart, mind, and spirit are tossed and turned—my emotions controlling me. Just yesterday, Larry said something, and my first thought was, "Oh, he's always so negative. That's so like him. He never thinks anything I say is worth anything." My heart believed it had every right to snap back telling him how wrong he was. And snap I did. "Larry, you always think negatively. What am I? Stupid and don't know anything? Maybe you're wrong."

My reaction felt completely justified because sometimes he does respond negatively. I had fallen back into my perfectionistic tendency of "all or nothing." My emotional rollercoaster used "absolute words" like never, always, all the time, and completely. I couldn't see or acknowledge anything good. My instability attacked Larry with contempt and blame.

As I wallowed in my distress, I became convinced I was hopeless because I said I wouldn't respond like that again. Then I became depressed because God can't possibly still love me. I keep doing the same old bad thing.

It took me awhile to acknowledge what I didn't want to face: Larry isn't negative *all the time,* and he does love and care about me. I wasn't trusting God in those moments because I only looked to Larry for his opinion of me, not God's. Then I heard God's whisper in my spirit: *Aren't you being negative too?* I acknowledged my failure and asked both God and Larry to forgive me. They graciously did.

Oh, how Satan weaves a tapestry wrapping us in overwhelming emotions. How can we have stability while being human, especially as "emotional" women? We want to glorify God. How can we?

What Motivates Instability?

In the quick moment before we sin, it doesn't seem like we're being motivated by anything. We're just—reacting, well—like a human being.

Author Jen Pollock Michel writes, "There is a biblical case for wanting, and wanting well ... Although easily corrupted, desire is good, right and necessary. It is a force of movement in our lives, a means of transportation. It can be the very thing that motivates us to change and that carries us to God. Growing into maturity doesn't mean abandoning our desires, but growing in our discernment of them."[23]

Satan uses our "wanting" to lure us into ungodly motives which fuel sinful choices. Another way to think of a motive is the word "desire," which the Bible uses a lot. Interestingly, after James' words in chapter 1:5-8 about being tossed and turned, James continues the discussion in chapter 1 with verses 13-15 by pointing to the underlying working of desires in our hearts.

> Let no one say when he is tempted, "I am being tempted by God," for God cannot be tempted with evil, and he himself tempts no one. But each person is tempted when he is lured and enticed by his own desire. Then desire when it has conceived gives birth to sin, and sin when it is fully grown brings forth death.

The word "enticed" means "caught by bait." Fishermen put out a particular bait attractive to the particular fish he wants. Satan knows what each attractive "alluring" and "enticing" bait is for each of us. So does our loving Master. He wants us to learn what our attractive "bait" is through the Holy Spirit's enlightenment about our motives.

My lack of emotional strength often results from my desires demanding affirmation of my value, assurance I'm loved, and attention so that I'm not ignored. If I don't direct my "wanting" to trusting God's supply, I crumble emotionally.

That's what happened to the disciples.

> On that day, when evening had come, he [Jesus] said to them, "Let us go across to the other side." And leaving the crowd, they took him with them in the boat, just as he was. And other boats were with him. And a great windstorm arose, and the waves were breaking into the boat, so that the boat was already filling. But he was in the stern, asleep on the cushion. And they woke him and said to him, "Teacher, do you not care that we are perishing?" And he awoke and rebuked the wind and said to the sea, "Peace! Be still!" And the wind ceased, and there was a great calm. He said to them, "Why are you so afraid? Have you still no faith?" And they were filled with great fear and said to one another, "Who then is this, that even the wind and the sea obey him?" Mark 4:35-41

I can surely understand the disciples' terror. There truly was a reason for fear. Even though most of them were seasoned fishermen, this storm was obviously way beyond their comfort zone. And because most of them were seasoned fishermen, they knew the danger. They knew fishermen who had perished in storms like this. The Sea of Galilee was famous for sudden windstorms. The boat was not just taking on water—it was "already filling." As they looked around for help, what did they see? Jesus asleep on a cushion. The man who should have been the first to take care of them was completely oblivious to their need and fear.

I can only imagine how "they woke him." Did they jostle him? The boat was already being jostled. Did they call to him? The sounds of the wind were already screaming. Did they grab him and shake him? That's what I would have done. Out of terror.

Then the disciples reveal their underlying motive. "Teacher, don't you care we are perishing? We thought we could depend upon you, yet obviously your own comfort—your sleep—is more important than us."

How poignant, especially coming from men. We women are more prone to ask, "Please tell me you love me." For these men to get in touch with their heart's cry is astounding. Most men would have just demanded Jesus remove the storm, not reveal their emotions.

I think their question is often what our heart is crying out to know: do you care? We can be tempted to express it through emotional outbursts because we're afraid we'll hear, "No, I don't care because you don't deserve it." I've been guilty of getting angry at Larry and only later realizing my heart was crying out, "Show me you love me! Maybe my anger, distress, or craziness will get your attention. Prove you care about my welfare!"

After Jesus calms the storm and the danger is past, the disciples are filled with wonder and awe. They rightly ask, *who is this who* can calm the wind and sea? If they had asked that question at the beginning, they wouldn't have become distressed. Because the answer is: "This is no surprise to Jesus. Even though he seems to be asleep on a cushion, he hasn't stopped loving us or caring for us because he is the powerful and omniscient God. We can trust whatever reason he is allowing this." Then God is glorified. When we allow stress to rule our lives, we are doubting the truth about Jesus' power and the Father's love. Then God isn't glorified.

Instability Starts Early

While in third grade, I angrily chased a girl on the playground and tripped. I fell on my face, shattering my top two front permanent teeth. I clearly remember thinking later, "God allowed that to happen. He can't be trusted." Each and every one of us experiences events birthing distrust of God and the resulting emotional instability.

In our lay counseling, and in the book my husband, Larry, and I wrote, *Never Ever Be the Same*, we use a model for answering the question, "Why do I do what I do?" It's our premise each of us as children (including the teenage years) experience painful (physical/ sexual, emotional, spiritual and mental) challenges which we are unable to correctly evaluate. In those moments, wanting God's glory isn't our desire.

From the pain, we receive a "message" which most often is a lie. More painful experiences solidify the lie, and Satan's messages becomes a part of our belief system. Because we want to avoid the pain of the lie, we create an avoidance reaction, which deepens into a self-protective, sinful strategy. We are convinced our strategy will keep us safe. When our strategy is threatened, we respond in a sinful way which we call "being hooked."

Here's a summary:

Wound (traumatic event): abuse, neglect, hurtful words, contempt, anger, being blamed unjustly, etc.

Message (lie): "you are worthless," "you never do anything right," "no one loves you," "you're not important enough for me to help you," etc.

Belief (distorted self-image or false opinion): "people can't be trusted," "don't even try, it won't work," "shut down my heart," "I'm stupid," "I'm on my own," etc.

Vow (commitment to avoid pain): "I'll never let anyone do that to me again," "if I'm dependable, no one will know I'm bad," "don't feel; just stuff any feelings" etc.

Strategy (defensive plan leaving out trust in God): anger, perfectionism, procrastination, passive aggressiveness, critical spirit, etc.

Hooking (any response the opposite of the fruit of the Spirit, Galatians 5:22-23): withdrawal, hate, discontentment, worry, anger, lack of self-control, contempt, etc.

The goal of identifying our wounds is not to blame the person responsible for the wound. We can never say, "Well, no wonder I'm making wrong choices. It's his fault. If he hadn't done that to me, I wouldn't be doing this."

That is not the purpose of identifying our wounds. The purpose is to call attention to how we decided, as children or teenagers, or really at any time in our lives, to deal with the wound and protect ourselves. Protecting ourselves from pain becomes the motive for our choices. We may not always discover the underlying causes for being hooked, but we are still accountable before God for calling upon him for help to live a godly life.

I had the privilege of guiding Abigail into these ideas. She shared:

My younger sister was favored because she was smarter than me. One time, my sister seemed to intentionally trip me as I walked down the hall. I bumped into a little table and a glass decorative bottle broke on the floor. My mother called to me and when I stood before her, she said, 'What did you do wrong?'

When I tried to explain what happened, my mother just shrugged and told me to finish the dishes. I felt voiceless since I couldn't explain it wasn't my fault. I was never believed even though I tried to be a good girl. I told myself, 'Abby, what a misfit you are. You're never good at anything. And God doesn't care. He doesn't help you.'

Whenever Abigail thought she displeased anyone, it crushed her. As a result, Abigail said, "I'm sorry" constantly. She felt weary trying to please everyone.

As we worked together over a period of time, she identified her effort to receive the approval she never had. A light-bulb moment occurred when she said, "I guess I need to be strong for everyone else so I'll feel worthwhile and valuable. I don't ask God for his directions; I just say yes to everyone. No wonder I get stressed out. People only help me when I'm overwhelmed."

Most importantly, she began to believe the truth: God did care for her even when it felt like he was asleep in the boat as life swirled around her in huge storms.

Just recently she said *no* to a co-worker who routinely took advantage of her. She prayed for wisdom. Then she knew she could risk obeying God because his love for her would never change—even if her co-worker hated her.

The next time you feel distressed in any way—anger, grief, depression, discouragement—ask Jesus, "Do you really care I'm sinking here?" The answer may not be immediate, but look for his caring love. Examine the underlying lies you believed as a child. Choose to believe the truth regardless of your emotions.

Psalm 62:1-2 assures you,

> For God alone my soul waits in silence;
> from him comes my salvation.
> He alone is my rock and my salvation,
> my fortress; I shall not be greatly shaken.

Worry

Let's use worry as an example of one of the many ways we become emotionally unstable, losing an opportunity to glorify God. The following ideas can apply to any number of unstable reactions. Just think of your "go-to" sinful reaction.

To get a sense of what people think about worry, I posted on Facebook: "Survey: do you think worry is a sin?" The response was immediate and abundant. Here are examples of the different categories of responses:

- I personally do not think it's sin. I think it's human nature for everyone to worry. Yes, sometimes we worry too much, but we can't really control it.

- Sometimes we have an instant gut reaction of worry. If we move in there and set up camp, yeah, it's sin. It means we've forgotten who is in charge.

- Yes, I believe worry is a sin, but we can recognize it, confess, and seek God's power.

- When you worry, you can't pray.

- Oh, please! Do we have to judge people or ourselves because we worry? It is human nature. Some worry more than others, but I am not going to call it sin.

- It depends upon your definition of worry. Is concern worry? Is fear worry? Is a prayer burden worry?

I may have been unfair to my Facebook friends because the word "worry" has different meanings and I admit I have my own definition. Because of what I believe Scripture says, I call worry sin. And for me, worry is distrust of God as I try to take control.

Yet, when circumstances assail us, we have three choices: fear, concern, and worry.

Fear is a legitimate reaction to real danger. If a bear is charging you, don't say, "Oh, I'm not worried, I'll just trust the Lord." God would say, "Take action."

Concern is based on legitimate danger but there's no opportunity for action. When your husband is late from work, he's not responding to your phone calls, and you see on the news there's a major accident on the same freeway your husband uses, you should be concerned. Your godly response is to pray.

At the point of fear and concern, it's possible to stay trusting in God. We may still have physical reactions: heart racing, palms sweaty, adrenaline coursing through us. Thoughts may even be bouncing around in our mind considering different options. At that point, we haven't sinned. We are being tempted but we are resisting worry and distrust of God. Jesus was tempted in the wilderness with thoughts of disobeying his Father. But he rejected them with the truth. Jesus stayed sinless for the purpose of being our perfect sacrifice.

Worry is when we lose trust in God. We become hopeless or decide God has deserted us. We believe God doesn't know what he's doing and we persist in rejecting his guidance. We might not credit God for any help available. It is sinful because we're telling God he doesn't know what he's doing.

The Lies Cheering for Worry

Any number of lies motivate us to distrust God and slide into worry. Here are some.

Worry is "normal," a part of being "human," therefore it's beyond our control. It may be true worry is natural and "being human," but it's not beyond our control. As Christians, God provides the power to live supernaturally and resist our fallen human nature, though often imperfectly. God provides everything we need to live a godly life (2 Peter 1:3) to his credit.

"A little worry" is acceptable. But when is it "too much"? Romans 14:23 says, *For whatever does not proceed from faith is sin.* "Whatever" means everything, big or little. Philippians 4:6 exhorts us, *do not be anxious about anything, but in everything by prayer and supplication with thanksgiving let your requests be made known to God.* Did you notice "anything" and "everything"? There's no "a little worry is acceptable."

If I worry, I'm hopeless. Satan whispers, "You said you wouldn't worry anymore but you keep doing it." But any and all sins can be forgiven. Our repentance draws us back to trust in God's gracious heart. We'll then grow in strength to resist the temptation next time.

Since we're calling worry a sin, let's be clear about what sin is. Anything can be sin if God is left out of it, even the "good" things we do. If our motive is about self, we are leaving out God. If we're not turning back to Jesus over and over again in the midst of temptation, it is sin.

Ian Major Thomas writes, "Sin therefore is exposed simply by relating our behavior to God's behavior. God is perfect, and by that perfection you and I can recognize sin, because sin is anything which falls short of His perfection.

"Sin also is defined in the Bible as faithless independence: 'Whatever is not from faith is sin' (Romans 14:23). It is an attitude of lawlessness' (I John 3:4)."[24]

What Motivates Our Worry?

Worry can be motivated by several heart commitments.

- *Worry helps me feel like I know what's best. I don't like feeling I'm not smart.* Every time we worry, we're basically saying we know better than God. Sara worries constantly about her children. She believes any difficulty is not good for them. Her worry, which she calls prayer, tells God what to do. She experienced very painful things in her childhood, so she has to convince God challenges aren't good for her children. But James 1:17 assures us, *Every good gift and every perfect gift is from above, coming down from the Father of lights with whom there is no variation or shadow due to change.*

- *Worry helps me feel powerful. I don't like feeling out of control.* I grew up hearing, "Why, of course worry works. What I worry about doesn't happen." It's a humorous saying but it shows how we're trying to impotently control circumstances rather than trusting the most powerful potentate there is. The next time you are tempted to worry, ask God, "Am I demanding my own way to feel powerful?" Many of us grew up feeling voiceless. Feeling powerful seems to demand we be heard.

- *Worry helps me feel included. I don't like feeling left out.* When something threatening occurs to those I love, and I'm not being included, Satan whispers, "I guess they don't think you're very important." I can text or email and say, "I was worried about you," with the hope they'll respond. We're depending upon another for what God wants to provide.

- *Worry helps me feel helpful. I can say I was a part of it.* This is closely aligned to the previous motives with a twist. I may tell others I've been praying but if it's motivated by worry, I might be expecting someone to point out the powerful prayer partner I've been. Then she should really say, "Thank you for worrying."

In each of these situations, the Holy Spirit is eager to reveal our motives and empower us to resist worry.

God Is Not Distressed About Our Distress

Will it seem strange if I say our weaknesses and potential for distress are actually a part of God's plan? Martin Luther wrote in *The Heidelberg Disputation*, "It is certain that man must utterly despair of his own ability before he is prepared to receive the grace of Christ."[25] Luther is first referring to our salvation but the principle applies to sanctification.

Our potential for emotional failure is God's way to create a need for him. We can be assured Jesus doesn't condemn us for our struggle or lack of faith. He always stands ready to not only forgive and restore us to fellowship, but cheer us on to victory.

Psalm 103:8-14 comforts us:

The Lord is merciful and gracious,
slow to anger and abounding in steadfast love.
He will not always chide,
nor will he keep his anger forever.
He does not deal with us according to our sins,
nor repay us according to our iniquities.
For as high as the heavens are above the earth,
so great is his steadfast love toward those who fear him;
as far as the east is from the west,
so far does he remove our transgressions from us.
As a father shows compassion to his children,
so the Lord shows compassion to those who fear him.
For he knows our frame;
he remembers that we are dust.

While on earth, Jesus sought out the weak and struggling. Those who claimed they were strong, like the Pharisees, he reprimanded. He didn't respond out of spite, but in an effort to shake them out of their deceived slumber. We should heed Paul's words in I Corinthians 1:26-31:

> For consider your calling, brothers: not many of you were wise according to worldly standards, not many were powerful, not many were of noble birth. But God chose what is foolish in the world to shame the wise; God chose what is weak in the world to shame the strong; God chose what is low and despised in the world, even things that are not, to bring to nothing things that are, so that no human being might boast in the presence of God. And because of him you are in Christ Jesus, who became to us wisdom from God, righteousness and sanctification and redemption, so that, as it is written, "Let the one who boasts, boast in the Lord."

Because God has chosen you in your weakness and sinful tendencies, you can boast in him. The more you look to him in your moments of distress, the more he will be glorified by the help he gives you.

Should I Shut Off My Feelings?

Sometimes it seems easier to deal with our emotional instability by denying our feelings or trying to actively not feel. Unfortunately, this tactic will only birth more difficulties. God makes it clear in the Psalms that expressing feelings is not only acceptable but healthy. Feelings themselves are not sin; it's what we do with them.

Tremper Longman III, professor and author, writes, "I already understood that the lament psalms [sic] gave me permission to complain to God. God invites us to speak to him with utter honesty and boldness. This is different from grumbling against him, as the Israelites did when they journeyed from Egypt to the Promised Land

(Num. 11). The Israelites spoke about God behind his back—or so they thought. Conversely, the complaints of the psalmists are spoken directly to God. And whereas the wilderness generation had given up on God, the psalmists had not. Even though they often addressed God in anger, they spoke to him, asking for help and hoping that he would answer them in their distress."[26]

Professor Longman makes an important distinction between grumbling and honest sharing. Grumbling is responding in distress without faith and trust. The righteous sharing of feelings is motivated by wanting to develop more trust in God.

You are not stealing from God's glory by expressing your emotions. In fact, trying to press down your feelings is like putting lava back into a volcano. The boiling lava will erupt at times which seem beyond your control and in inappropriate ways. You may not even be aware of the underlying cause and as a result wonder, "What motivated *that*?"

God has created the Body of Christ as a caring community where we can share our struggles, temptations, and even our distress. There should be no shame in exploring our emotions. In the sharing, we discover our motives and are healed. That's what happened for Brenda.

I met Brenda at a women's retreat. As we sat amongst the beautiful forest of the mountain conference center, she tearfully explained, "I'm so worried and stressed I'll never have grandchildren. My only child, my son, and his wife don't want children. I know I shouldn't complain to them but I can't help myself. I want to trust God but it feels like a terrible loss."

I asked her, "Brenda, tell me about your childhood."

She told me several things and then said, "I loved my grandmother Mimi so much. She seemed to favor me. She talked a lot about how important family is. One time she said something like, 'At the end of the day, only family will stand by you. And if you don't have family, you're nothing.'"

"Remember what I talked about this morning about the vow? Did you make any vow after hearing that?"

"I remember thinking something like, 'I better make sure I have a family.' And of course, I did."

"Yes, you have a son but because your family line may not continue, does it say anything about your worth and value? Remember the words your Mimi said?"

"Yeah, she said, 'you're nothing.'" Brenda's face showed shock. "Am I overreacting with worry and control because it feels like I'm nothing without my family continuing? My Mimi didn't mean that but as a little girl I guess I took it that way."

"Does that seem true?"

"Yeah, I guess so. I guess I'm overreacting because it feels like my value is threatened. No wonder I'm not trusting God. But I want to."

Brenda was willing to pray and ask for God's forgiveness for her sinful worry and for rejecting God's value of her. As she walked away, I could tell her distress had been lifted.

When you are distressed, ask God to reveal the underlying causes of your reactions.

Woman with Issue of Blood
Mark 5:24b-34

This nameless woman had no hope. During twelve long years, she had taken every possible step to become well. Her bloody discharge made her ceremonially unclean, unable to enter the temple and worship her God. Her husband must have left her long ago because he couldn't touch her without becoming unclean himself.

She had spent every cent she had. She had put her hope in numerous doctors. In fact, Mark 5:26 says, *who had suffered much under many physicians, and had spent all that she had, and was no better but rather grew worse.* Had doctors taken advantage of her? Had they offered hope when there was no hope? Had they promised a cure and taken her money, yet had no clue what to do?

Regardless of all her efforts, she was still an outcast. She must have felt distressed walking the street looking for any sign of hope.

We don't know when she first heard of Jesus. Was there a rumor about what he was doing—healing people—or as she walked did she notice he was there? Hope must have filled her heart. Or did the renewed hope quickly drain out of her. *There is no hope. Why even try? Yet try I must. Jesus is my last hope.*

She stealthily looked around her. When no one was watching, she reached out and touched the hem of his garment, possibly terrified of being called out for public humiliation. She risked making this godly man unclean. Yet her distress was so great, she had to try.

And Jesus, perceiving in himself that power had gone out from him, immediately turned about in the crowd and said, "Who touched my garments?" And his disciples said to him, "You see the crowd pressing around you, and yet you say, 'Who touched me?'" And he looked around to see who had done it. But the woman, knowing what had happened to her, came in fear and trembling and fell down before him and told him the whole truth. And he said to her, "Daughter, your faith has made you well; go in peace, and be healed of your disease." Mark 5:30-34

I hear concern in Jesus' voice, not anger. Of course, he knows who touched him; he's omniscient God. Yet he knows it will be healthy for her to express her distress and publicly acknowledge his provision.

The disciples on the other hand were most likely hassled and frustrated. Their attempts at crowd control were futile. They may have been distressed feeling responsible to protect their teacher. Now someone was not only interrupting their next appointment—slowing them down—someone had touched him without their knowing. Were they placing him in danger?

After her touch, knowing she was well, she approached with "fear and trembling." What will happen now? Will he only dismiss her with cruel words or call for the priests to take away an unclean woman who polluted others? She feels prompted to tell him the whole truth publicly, so great was her relief. *I'm healed! I know it. I feel it! Oh Jesus, thank you.* What she longed and prayed for twelve years had been fulfilled.

Her fears are alleviated as Jesus calls her Daughter and acknowledges her courage in reaching out. His voice had to have been tender and inviting, understanding and gentle. Then he assures her of complete healing, not just the cessation of her discharge. She'll never have to feel hopeless or unclean again.

Because of her distress, Jesus is glorified.

Reflection and Discussion Questions

1. What kind of distress do you experience most often? In those moments, what feels at risk?

2. Do you think worry is sin? Why or why not?

3. How does it feel to identify times you might be "like a wave of the sea driven and tossed by the wind"?

4. What is your philosophy about "desires" (James 1:14-15)? Does it seem like you shouldn't have them? What do you like about them and what do you dislike?

5. When have you felt like Jesus was asleep in your life's sinking boat? What happened?

6. When Jesus calms a storm in your life, what does your acknowledgment of him identify?

7. Have you ever thought about how we learn instability early in life? What are your ideas?

8. What is most important to you about the "model" of how we are hooked?

9. What is your most traumatic childhood experience?

10. What lies about worry have you succumbed to?

11. What motivates your worry most often?

12. How did you feel reading God is not distressed by your distress?

13. What did you take away as most important about the story of the woman with the issue of blood?

Chapter 7
Self-Controlled
Choose Wisely

Don't just fight harder against the temptation; instead yield more fully to His life."[27]—Jennifer Kennedy Dean

We hide behind our carefully crafted masks and reputations, worried and defensive about anything that could blow our cover...The mistake at the root of this unwinnable game is, of course, that approval is not ours to win. We have already been acknowledged.[28]—Rebecca Konyndyk

I'm the worst possible person to write this chapter.
I am very self-controlled.
Do those two true statements seem incongruent?
I can understand if they do. But the truth is, I'm the worst possible person to write on self-control, even though I'm very self-controlled, because in a large part my motives aren't for God's glory, they are for my self-protection. The self-control the Bible talks about isn't intended to be about "self," its purpose is to empower us to

obey God. I've been a very self-controlled person empowered by my determination to not allow my perceived faults to be seen.

Moments after I was molested as an eight-year-old, I thought, "Kathy, you should have prevented that. You are a dirty little girl." Of course, the message was a lie, but I believed it was true. I never told anyone what happened. My heart sat for years in the agony of shame, vowing to protect myself from experiencing another incident of emotional pain. I learned to be hyper-vigilant, constantly evaluating the behavior and feelings of others to determine whether they had destructive motives toward me. My goal was to make sure no one touched me inappropriately again.

When I was in third grade, about the same time as the molestation, I said something mean to a classmate and several students heard me. They called to our teacher, Mrs. Leighton, and she came over. Mrs. Leighton was my Princess in Shining Armor. I was her teacher's pet. I could do no wrong, and she favored me. I felt special and important. When the students reported what I'd said, Mrs. Leighton asked me with a worried look on her face, "Kathy, did you say that?" To keep my favored status, I replied, "No, Mrs. Leighton, I didn't say that." Mrs. Leighton walked away with a satisfied look on her face.

I knew I'd lied and hated the feeling of being a liar—and everyone knowing I was. If I'd known about being able to ask Jesus to forgive me, I could have thrown off the heavy mantle of self-judgement. I didn't.

But without knowing what I was doing, I did know how to form a self-protective strategy of dependability. *The way to make sure no one knows I'm a liar is to always be dependable—to stay in control of everything I do to appear dependable.*

When I was ten years old, I sat with a group of my relatives and loved hearing the bantering back and forth. My Aunt Nita suddenly commented, "Oh, look at Kathy. Isn't she sitting so nicely, just like a poised young lady." Oh my! A flood of approval swept over me. I certainly wasn't dirty and a liar in that moment. The praise felt so good to my thirsty, guilty soul. I added another layer of dependability dressed up as self-control: be poised. *Hopefully someone will compliment me and I'll feel good about myself.*

My layers of self-control were formed by many other experiences. If my self-control slipped, I felt exposed. I was terrified of being identified as dirty, a liar, imperfect, or discourteous. The solution in my young brain produced people-pleasing, worry, and so many of the issues we have been exploring in this book, which exclude God's glory.

You may not have had similar experiences or be motivated by the same strategies, but all of us find godly self-control to be a challenge in some area of life. My belief was confirmed when I took an informal survey on Facebook. Knowing self-control is mentioned as one of the fruit of the Spirit, I asked, "Of the fruit of the Spirit, (love, joy, peace, patience, kindness, goodness, faithfulness, gentleness, self-control) please list the three 'fruit' you have the most trouble with, putting them in order of difficulty."

Of the approximately thirty responses I received, self-control came in a very close second to patience. But when you think about these attributes, you need self-control to live in any of the Spirit's fruit. Godly self-control can be defined as obeying God when my inclinations and desires want something other than what he wants. When we love, have joy, are peaceful, patient, kind, good, faithful, and gentle, we have chosen in God's power to obey him and respond as he would.

Who Takes the Cake for Lack of Self-Control?

When we think of lack of control in biblical characters, we most often think of impulsive Peter. He was opinionated, thought he was always right, and never thought before he acted.

But Jesus knew the plans he had for Peter and guess who wrote about self-control? Peter. *Therefore, preparing your minds for action, and being sober-minded, set your hope fully on the grace that will be brought to you at the revelation of Jesus Christ* (I Peter 1:13).

The word *sober-minded* is another way to describe self-control. Author and commentator Kenneth Wuest defines it as "to be calm and collected in spirit, to be temperate, dispassionate, circumspect. It speaks of the proper exercise of the mind, that state of mind in which the individual is self-controlled and is able to see things without the distortion caused by worry, fear, and their related attitudes."[29]

Unfortunately, our "self" control is not always empowered by the Holy Spirit. It can be a protective means of controlling life thus disobeying God believing his invitation is too risky. We revert to the strategies we learned as children to protect ourselves from feeling the pain—whatever it was. The Bible describes those strategies as "the flesh." Jennifer Kennedy Dean writes, "Our flesh likes to be in control. Of everything. In control of ourselves, in control of the people around us, in control of our circumstances, in control of other people's circumstances. Nothing will throw our flesh into a bigger revolt than when we realize we have to hand over control. It's a death blow to our pride."[30]

Jennifer continues, "The impulse of our flesh is to try harder, manage more, enforce our will more stringently, maneuver and massage and finesse until we get everyone and everything straightened out and marching to our beat."[31]

Galatians 5:16-17 describes Spirit-control. *But I say, walk by the Spirit, and you will not gratify the desires of the flesh. For the desires of the flesh are against the Spirit, and the desires of the Spirit are against the flesh, for these are opposed to each other, to keep you from doing the things you want to do.*

As the flesh is tempting us, we can walk by the Spirit in three primary ways: captivate our thoughts, cross-examine our motives, and confront our greatest fear. Let's look at each one.

Captivate Our Thoughts

Yesterday morning at 6 a.m., as I walked home from our neighborhood work-out room, I felt drained by the unusual humidity along with the 90-degree temperature. I decided, "Tomorrow morning, I'll have to drive the car." And then the most delicious thought entered my mind. "After I finish, I'll go get a donut."

Oh! What motivation to drive the car to the gym. I'm always looking for any reason to get sweets. I felt delightfully sneaky. Larry would never know what I'd done because he slept late. Oh, I could already taste my favorite donut—the sugar cinnamon spice. *What does it matter I'm trying to eat more healthfully? I deserve a donut! Just one won't hurt anything. God, it's no big deal, right?*

Then my spiritual eyes were opened and 2 Corinthians 10:5 came to mind: *We destroy arguments and every lofty opinion raised against the knowledge of God, and take every thought captive to obey Christ.*

I saw Satan's ploy to destroy my self-control by using a tactic of mine from childhood. I often felt like the possibilities offered me were promises. Most often they were not fulfilled. I shared a room with my sister and always wanted my own room. At one point, most likely when I was a pre-teen, my mother mentioned, "Daddy and I are thinking of making the garage into your own bedroom." What great news. I felt important and valued.

Emotionally, I waited on the edge of my seat for the next mention of the coming transformation. But my parents never brought up the idea again. In my insecurity, I didn't ask about it because I feared hearing, "We aren't going to do it." Such an answer would feel like rejection and they had finally discovered the truth: *I'm a dirty little girl who lies and I don't deserve something special.* As long as I didn't ask, I could keep the hope alive I wasn't shameful, insignificant, and unlovable. In a sense, I kept hope alive through controlling my mind to think positively.

My hope died a slow painful death, and I'm sure my parents thought I'd forgotten. Even though I'd tried to keep the promise alive through never asking, I felt terrible regardless. I wasn't important because they didn't even remember mentioning it.

Somehow in my complicated way of thinking, I began to hate being disappointed, even by myself. My belief was "a broken promise equals rejection." My warped "self-control" could make sure I kept any promise to myself of a highly desired thing. *I can't control other people but I can control myself.*

I know this story must sound unbelievably strong. I didn't know Satan was attacking me constantly with shame. Heather Davis Nelson writes, "At its core, shame is fear of weakness, failure, or unworthiness being unveiled for all to see, or fear that at least one other person will notice that which we want to hide ... Shame commonly masquerades as embarrassment, or the nagging sense of 'not quite enough.'"[32] Heather also explains the difference between guilt and shame. Guilt is "I did something bad." Shame is "I am bad."

I believed both. I believed the lie *I did something shameful* because I didn't prevent the molestation. I also believed the lie *I am bad.* The molestation and so many other attacks had done their damage.

All this was involved yesterday morning when I promised myself a donut. But I was willing to allow God to empower me to *take every thought captive to obey Christ* (2 Corinthians 10:5). *Kathy, if you continue to promise yourself this, by tomorrow morning, it'll be even harder to resist.* Any semblance of Spirit control would be hidden under layers of "But you promised and if you don't come through, you'll feel rejected." Praise God, I saw the lies and I refused to be caught in Satan's web.

As I studied the truth of 2 Corinthians 10:5, I began to envision any thought as an arrow headed toward my heart and mind. Previously, I always believed any thought was generated by me; therefore, I had already succumbed to sin. Constantly bombarded by thoughts, I felt discouraged. I felt like the little dirty girl.

When we invite a sinful thought arrow in, our motive is to provide for ourselves. In a way, we are "self-controlled" by using our sinful power to go in the wrong direction. Any choice we make is controlled by something. We are motivated to obey God because we believe he'll provide something good or we are motivated to disobey because we believe he won't provide what we need—and we must.

Remember Eve? She ate the fruit because she believed the arrow of Satan's lie: *But the serpent said to the woman, "You will not surely die. For God knows that when you eat of it your eyes will be opened, and you will be like God, knowing good and evil"* (Genesis 3:4-5). Satan's message? "God is withholding something you deserve and need. He really doesn't want your best, but I do." For me that morning, Satan was saying, "God couldn't possibly be withholding something good like a donut. Just think how good it will taste."

Each of us, when we're motivated to provide for ourselves, have a choice whether it's food, illicit sex, gossiping, or any other sin. Every time we disobey, we are motivated by demanding something we *think* will be good for us.

By captivating our thoughts and evaluating whether it's a lie or truth, plus asking for the Spirit's power, we choose obedience resulting in God's power being seen by others.

Cross-Examine Our Motives

I recently received an email from a missionary friend, Kaylee, who I had the privilege of giving soul care to before she went overseas. She wrote:

That amazing outreach occurred while I was in a personal funk. When God worked in spite of my inadequacy, I realized how much I fear not being in control, and how not admitting that fear closes me off from the Father. I recognized when an uncontrollable person or a situation frustrates me, I criticize it and then distance myself. I don't want to feel disapproved. In previous low times, I could build myself up doing more "good" and spiritual things like reading my Bible more. But I saw then I only wanted to feel better not glorify God. My motives were definitely mixed like you talk about, Kathy. This time, I had none of that.

I remembered you talking about how our childhood experiences affect our motives. I asked the Lord to bring to mind how I learned to find comfort in spiritual exercises rather than God. I may have shared this with you. As a missionary kid while on the field, my parents wanted to appear strong spiritually. We kids had to perform and not let anyone know of our struggles. Mom and Dad had a spiritual pat answer for everything. "Just give it to

God." "Pray more." "Trust the Lord." "Control yourself." I learned quickly to earn their approval through spiritual activity and giving the acceptable responses. I wasn't motivated to please God, only to make sure I didn't shame my parents and the ministry. I feared my parents being unhappy with me.

Now the Lord has been helping me to risk going more deeply. In the funk I was in and God working regardless, I saw my desire to serve or ability to contribute had no bearing on the amazing work God did. I became willing to experience a lack of control and cooperate with whatever God called me to do even if uncomfortable. This time I didn't have to just give the spiritual answers. I actually shared my struggle with others.

I so appreciated Kaylee's heart for wanting God's glory and being willing to "cross-examine" her motives and become purified. Unfortunately, like Kaylee indicated, we can depend upon pat answers and slogans rather than looking below the waterline to our motives and the lies fueling them.

Here are some questions to ask yourself to cross-examine motives. There is no particular order.

- Do I have anything selfish to gain from this choice?

- What do I want to avoid being seen as/like?

- What does that person's reaction or behavior seem to say about me?

- What would my disobedience say about God's nature and the way he works?

- How does this situation or that person's response remind me of my childhood?

- How do I want to respond that is similar to the way I responded as a child?

- If I obey God, what might he want to accomplish for me or for others resulting in his glory? What would his glory possibly look like?

- If I disobey God, what might be the consequences?

- Do I feel like God is treating me like that dangerous person did during my childhood?

- What is the most hurtful thing anyone has ever said or done to me?

These questions are for you to ask yourself (or reword to ask others as we'll see in the Sensitive Chapter) to help you get in touch with your motives. Let me give you some examples.

- *What do I hope to gain?*

Lily grew up in a family with three sisters, and the competition to be heard was fierce. She rarely felt like her opinion was heard or important. While in college, one teacher exclaimed, "You have a way with words." That statement seemed to affirm her value and birthed a selfish strength to control situations and relationships with talking.

Unfortunately, her many words only drove friends away because she talked about herself almost non-stop. Plus, she really thought she was bringing glory to God by sharing all the wonderful things he was doing in her life.

Lily began asking herself *What do I hope to gain?* The Holy Spirit revealed her demand to be heard and affirmed. Although difficult, she began recognizing more and more God's value for her thoughts and opinions, even if people couldn't receive them. It made a difference.

- *What do I hope to avoid?*

Mae told me, "When I was in middle school, my parents were always sleeping in on weekends because of their partying. If my brothers and I made too much noise, our parents came out and cursed at us. The most hurtful was when my mom yelled, 'You'll never amount to anything unless you learn to shut up.' I learned to control my every move—and my brothers'. Even now, too much noise makes me uncomfortable because I vowed to be quiet as a mouse so I wouldn't get yelled at.

"Now, when my two sons start rough-housing, I get panicky. I yell at them to be quiet. Isn't that ironic? I yell so they will be quiet."

In time, Mae allowed the Holy Spirit to help her relax more and more by seeing she didn't need to fear someone would yell at her. And even if they did, it didn't mean she would "never amount to anything."

- *How do I feel threatened?*

When Charlotte was a little girl she rode with her grandmother late one evening. She has a vague memory of being in the backseat of a big Plymouth where she could barely see over the front seat's high back.

It must have been around the 1950s when I was seven or eight. The car was stopped at the intersection, and my grandmother suddenly asked me, 'Is there a divided highway here?'

I had no idea what a divided highway was, but I'd learned I always had to answer a question. That was respecting my elders. So, I guessed and said, 'no.' Wrong answer. My grandmother drove forward and drove right into the curb of a divided highway. I still don't know why she asked me or why she couldn't see it, but I immediately thought, 'I'm so stupid. I should have known the right answer.'

Even today I have a hard time saying, 'I don't know.' My intelligence always feels threatened. As a result, I jump to conclusions to give any answer and I don't ask God first.

After Charlotte recognized the self-imposed wound of declaring herself stupid, she repented of her motive to protect herself. Now she can say, "I don't know." She's also more willing to seek God and give an answer based on what he says rather than what she thinks another person wants or needs to hear.

Confront Our Greatest Fear

Godly self-control is when we choose God's power to obey, even at the risk of what we fear, bringing him glory. After looking through the questions above of cross-examining your motives, can you identify what you fear the most? If confronting that fear and conquering it would bring God the most glory, would you be willing to face the fear, knowing he will provide what you need? Being willing to face such a risk will break its stronghold over you and strengthen you to obey God more.

As Larry and I give soul-care counseling to others, many have said something like, "If I obey God in that way, it'll feel like death." This is not a kind of needed "death" to our selfish flesh. This is a kind of death birthed in distrust of what God might do or allow. It feels like we'll be helpless to face the worst possible thing we fear. And guess what? We have all felt the same way. So here are some questions to ask yourself.

- Does it seem like being exposed as weak feels like death?

- Does it seem like being seen as stupid feels like death?

- Does it seem like forgiving your perpetrator feels like death?

- Does it seem like going against the opinion of a favored child feels like death?

- Does it seem like allowing consequences for a drug-addicted adult child feels like death?

I feel tense just listing those possibilities, because I have been faced with some of them. But wanting God's glory can motivate us to trust him enough to do what seems like possible death. Of course, not physical death but a spiritual or emotional death of our desires, beliefs, or strategies. When we do, we are surprised to see we survived and God brought something good out of it as he promises (Romans 8:28).

Being willing to face, confront and conquer our fear in God's power would seem to be related to Jesus' words in Luke 14:26-29, 33:

> If anyone comes to me and does not hate his own father and mother and wife and children and brothers and sisters, yes, and even his own life, he cannot be my disciple. Whoever does not bear his own cross and come after me cannot be my disciple. For which of you, desiring to build a tower, does not first sit down and count the cost, whether he has enough to complete it? ... So therefore, any one of you who does not renounce all that he has cannot be my disciple.

"Hating" means giving up our disordered love of something or someone which we have demanded. For example, safety, comfort, respect, love, etc.

"Bearing our own cross" means surrendering our own self-protection and trusting God's power to protect us. We stop trying to change people or circumstances and instead desire to change ourselves. This doesn't mean we don't take action, but our action is fueled by his power not our own "self" control.

"Counting the cost" means cross-examining our motives to see where we are not trusting God. We recognize God's sovereign hand in the people and circumstances he allows in our lives. We believe he intends challenges for our growth and good.

And in all these God is glorified.

Do we hate, bear, and count once and never again? Don't I wish. We'll continue that process over and over again until we rush into the arms of Jesus in heaven. But through all of it, we have this assurance: *Keep your life free from love of money, and be content with what you have, for he has said, "I will never leave you nor forsake you." So, we can confidently say, The Lord is my helper; I will not fear; what can man do to me?* Hebrews 13:5-6.

Robert Smith, Jr., Professor of Christian Preaching at Beeson Divinity School, Birmingham, Alabama, was faced with a real death yet his confidence stayed true.

On the evening of October 30, 2010, during an attempted robbery at the restaurant where his son, Tony, worked, Tony was shot. When Professor Smith received the phone call with the news, Professor Smith says, "I desperately asked God to save Tony's life and glorify himself. I had great aspirations for Tony. My prayer was that Tony be spared so he could serve God at a high level of consecration." An hour later another call gave him and his wife the horrible news—Tony, 34, had died.

He writes, "During the trial, I saw the back of Tony's murderer, then eighteen years old. I saw his mother and some family members weeping as the judge sentenced him to many years in prison. I prayed about my feelings toward and relationship with this young man.

"For forty-four years I have preached about the forgiveness that Joseph, Job, and Jesus extended to those who brought great pain in their lives. I knew how to explain, illustrate, and apply forgiveness from a biblical perspective. Now God was telling me if I really believed what I had been preaching, then I must, by his grace, live that forgiveness now."

Over time, God empowered Professor Smith to forgive. "Though the wound to my heart is still open, I have forgiven Tony's murderer. Jesus continues to redress my wound and is bringing me to progressive wholeness."

Professor Smith believed God wanted him to have contact with the young man and two years later, he was able to mail a letter he had been preparing for some time. He asked in his letter if the inmate would add his name to the visitors list so he could come in person and say, "Jesus loves and forgives you and so do I."

Two years later, four years after Tony died, the inmate put Professor Smith on his visitors list. "Soon by God's grace I will see the young man whose face was the last face our son saw before standing in the presence of the Lord. I will offer the young man the forgiveness that Christ offers to me and to all who will believe."[33]

Leprous Naaman
2 Kings 5:9-14

The story of leprous Naaman shows God's way of helping a proud man cross-examine his motives and confront his greatest fear.

So Naaman came with his horses and chariots and stood at the door of Elisha's house. And Elisha sent a messenger to him, saying, "Go and wash in the Jordan seven times, and your flesh shall be restored, and you shall be clean." But Naaman was angry and went away, saying, "Behold, I thought that he would surely come out to me and stand and call upon the name of the Lord his God, and wave his hand over the place and cure the leper. Are not Abana and Pharpar, the rivers of Damascus, better than all the waters of Israel? Could I not wash in them and be clean?" So he turned and went away in a rage. But his servants came near and said to him, "My father, it is a great word the prophet has spoken to you; will you not do it? Has he actually said to you, 'Wash, and be clean'?" 2 Kings 5:9-13

Naaman's pride would seem to be a protection against the shame of being seen as leprous. His pride is most likely based on his success as a general. He's depending upon his performance not his status as an image bearer of Jehovah. So, when Elisha doesn't cooperate with Naaman's demand to be treated with the respect he deserves, Naaman reacts out of control with anger. It's as if Naaman is saying, "I feel horrible about my condition, but don't you dare think I am horrible. I refuse to let anyone think of me as shameful. I deserve better. I'm angry because you haven't treated me well. You have a problem, not me."

Naaman's servants are wiser than he. They ask him a kind of "soul-care" question related to his motives. They basically ask, "What does it matter which river you wash in? What are you trying to protect? You are the same person regardless of where you wash. See yourself the way Jehovah God sees you as important and valuable. Elisha has promised God will heal you. Why would you spoil that?"

I admit I may be adding to their intentions. But God allows us to experience difficult things and asks, "Even if obeying me puts you in a position of emotional danger, will you let me heal you as I walk with you through dirty waters?"

Naaman was willing to humble himself, face the rebellion of his pride, and subject himself to what he feared—being viewed as someone only worthy of washing in a dirty river. And he is healed! *So he went down and dipped himself seven times in the Jordan, according to the word of the man of God, and his flesh was restored like the flesh of a little child, and he was clean* (vs. 14).

Child of God, do you wish to be healed and delivered from the lies which create a lack of self-control, hurting both yourself and others? Be willing to be exposed to what you fear. Take hold of God's power to obey. Use his power to reject your sinful inclinations and trust him enough to know he'll define your value and wipe away your shame.

Reflection and Discussion Questions

1. How would you describe or rate your level of self-control? Do you think it's empowered by yourself or the Holy Spirit most of the time?

2. Who in the Bible do you think had the least self-control? Besides Jesus, who had the most?

3. Of the fruit of the Spirit, which three do you have more trouble exhibiting?

4. When you do have Spirit-motivated self-control, to what do you attribute that?

5. What was your reaction to my story about wanting a room to myself?

6. What does Satan use most often as the lie fueling your lack of self-control?

7. What was your initial reaction to the "cross-examination questions?" Have you tried to use any of them since reading the chapter?

8. Do you relate to any of the examples (Lily, Mae, or Charlotte)?

9. What would be your story as you answer any of the questions from the examples of those women?

10. What is your greatest fear? On a scale of 1 to 10, ten being greatest, how would you rate it?

11. Can you define and/or share what God is calling you to do about your fear?

12. Can you give an example of facing a fear in the past and how God walked through it with you?

13. What did you find surprising and meaningful in Naaman's story?

Chapter 8

Struck with Awe
Praise God in Truth

A godly life is lived out of an astonished heart—a heart that is astonished at grace. We go to the Bible to be astonished, to be amazed at God and Christ and the cross and grace and the gospel.[34] —John Piper

In both the Old and New Testaments, the people of God experienced Him in various ways. As each need arose, they had the privilege of knowing their God in a novel way. God chose to reveal himself through his actions towards them, and they responded by describing Him with a new name. As we observe how our Biblical ancestors related to God in their specific need, we can also take heart that He will do the same for us.[35]—Pam Palagy

Jean Wilund shared on her blog.

Years ago, I found myself stuck in circumstances. So, I prayed. A lot. But nothing changed, except my joy. It evaporated. My patience began to run dry along with my joy. I decided I was done praying. I began praising instead. I stopped focusing on my situation and focused on all the great things God has done from the beginning of time.

I praised him for his unchanging, unfailing character—character trait by character trait. I praised him because he's worthy of praise all the time. As my praises rose, I experienced a startling development: my joy returned. I'd stumbled upon something.

Praise didn't change my circumstances, but it changed me. It brought me the joy of the Lord. As joy filled my heart and mind, I felt stronger in the midst of my circumstances. Truth overcame fear and doubt. Confident assurance of his unconditional love overwhelmed me. Peace rose up knowing he simply will not fail us.

I felt motivated, empowered, and excited to follow the Lord. Wherever he led.[36]

I'm sure those who noticed Jean's journey, plus those who read this account on her blog, were giving glory to God and were encouraged to praise him themselves.

Childhood Experiences Label God

We know God deserves our praise and his Word commands it, but we feel blocked. We can't figure out why. But there are reasons. Listen to J. I. Packer's story. He is Board of Governor's Professor of Theology at Regent College and author of more than forty books, including his bestseller *Knowing God*.

When Jesus Christ laid hold of me, I was already well on my way to becoming a cynic ...

Cynics are people who have grown skeptical about the goodness of life, and who look down on claims to sincerity, morality, and value....

I was reared in a stable home and did well at school, but, being an introvert, I was always shy and awkward in company. Also, I was barred from sports and team games by reason of a hole in my head—literally, just over the brain—that I had acquired in a road accident at age 7. For years I had to cover the hole, where there was no bone, by wearing an aluminum plate, secured to my head by elastic....

... So I developed a self-protective sarcasm, settled for low expectations from life, and grew bitter. Pride led me to stand up for Christian truth in school debates, but with no interest in God or a willingness to submit to him.[37]

Then Packer began studying Ecclesiastes. From chapters one through six, he identified Solomon's phrase, "under the sun," as meaning "the natural order, wisdom in itself, uninhabited self-indulgence, sheer hard work, money-making, public service, the judicial system, and pretentious religiosity." He had to agree with Solomon's point: living "under the sun" doesn't bring fulfillment because it is void of God's perspective.

Then one verse changed his cynicism: *He has made everything beautiful in its time. Also, he has put eternity into man's heart, yet so that he cannot find out what God has done from the beginning to the end* (3:11). Professor Packer defines "eternity" as "a desire to know, as God knows, how everything fits in with everything else to produce lasting value, glory, and satisfaction."

Packer points to Ecclesiastes 12:13: *The end of the matter; all has been heard. Fear God and keep his commandments, for this is the whole duty of man.* Professor Packer concluded, "Being too proud to enjoy the enjoyable is a very ugly shortcoming, and one that calls for immediate correction. Let it be acknowledged that, as I had to learn long ago, discovering how under God ordinary things can bring joy is the cure for cynicism."

Years after Professor Packer turned from his cynicism, he wrote, "What makes life worthwhile is having a big enough objective, something which catches our imagination and lays hold of our allegiance; and this the Christian has, in a way that no other man has. For what higher, more exalted, and more compelling goal can there be than to know God?"[38]

Professor Packer clearly shares where his cynicism began: his painful childhood. I know what you're thinking. "There she goes again, harping about my childhood. What's the big deal?"

I understand if this seems repetitious. But it's that important. We need to examine the impact of our wounding experiences because they laid a foundation impacting us to this day. And whether we formed cynicism, procrastination, anger, discontentment, or so many other possible self-protective sinful patterns, we have misinterpreted what God allowed in our lives and his nature. We should be praising him in awe for his loving work but instead we've developed distrust of him. Sometimes even active rebellion or a refusal to praise him.

Think of it this way. Many people say to us as we give them soul care counseling, "Oh, that was just the way my dad was. It didn't bother me that much. It was just the way things were."

We reply, "OK. Would you like your own daughter (or son, niece, nephew, or grandchild) at that age to experience what you did?"

"Oh, of course not. That would be so painful."

"What do you think it would make them think about themselves (or God, life, other people)?"

"Well, my daughter would be confused (or angry, or disappointed, etc.)."

"Then why was it ok for it to happen to you? And maybe you felt the same way but have buried the feelings?"

Usually the lightbulb comes on, and they see how painful it was. Our present-day response is based in years of any number of protective measures: denial, claiming to forgive, refusing to think about it, etc. But all we experience, good or bad, affects us. As I've stated, as children, we don't know how to think of it with a godly perspective. Very often we believe lies about God which can prevent us from knowing the truth about his greatness.

Some people also learn to try to pacify God as a means of protection. He's a scary God who didn't come through for us so we have to make him happy "just like I had to make my mom or dad, or abuser happy trying to protect myself." That's what occurred in Zechariah 7.

> In the fourth year of King Darius, the word of the Lord came to Zechariah on the fourth day of the ninth month, which is Chislev. Now the people of Bethel had sent Sharezer and Regem-melech and their men to entreat the favor of the Lord, saying to the priests of the house of the Lord of hosts and the prophets, "Should I weep and abstain in the fifth month, as I have done for so many years?" vss. 1-3

Do you hear their motive? They are seeking God's favor. They use a pride-based bribe. "God, have you seen our great religiosity? We've been doing exactly what you've asked therefore you owe us with favors." What would indicate that? God giving them what they want without any consideration of God's good plan.

Is God impressed? Here's his response: *Then the word of the Lord of hosts came to me [Zechariah]: "Say to all the people of the land and the priests, When you fasted and mourned in the fifth month and in the seventh, for these seventy years, was it for me that you fasted? And when you eat and when you drink, do you not eat for yourselves and drink for yourselves?* (vss. 4-6). These men weren't wanting God's glory nor trusting his pure heart of love for them. They didn't believe he would do the right thing. They must bribe him to demand what they want. They had heard the truth from their prophets but they still thought they had to earn his goodness. Without believing the truth about him, they weren't assured his motive was for their good. Yet God kindly and graciously reminds them of what pleases him.

> And the word of the Lord came to Zechariah, saying, "Thus says the Lord of hosts, Render true judgments, show kindness and mercy to one another, do not oppress the widow, the fatherless, the sojourner, or the poor, and let none of you devise evil against another in your heart." But they refused to pay attention and turned a stubborn shoulder and stopped their ears that they might not hear. (vss. 8-11)

God points out the ways he wants to be glorified as they represent his nature: he gives true judgements, shows kindness and mercy, doesn't oppress those in need, and never devises evil toward anyone. His heart is always purely motivated to bring good—what he knows is best.

Of course, we don't know their motives for resisting God's plans. We don't know their "childhood experiences." But their response can sure remind us of us. *They made their hearts diamond-hard lest they should hear the law and the words that the Lord of hosts had sent by his*

Spirit through the former prophets (vs. 12).

Diamond-hard? Oh my, that's hard. If God wanted to make his point strongly, there's no more impressive way to say it. A diamond is the hardest God-created substance on earth.

Zechariah 7 reveals God's heart and motive. He persists in reaching out to them because he wants to be known in truth. He persisted continuously throughout the conversation. If they had repented and turned to him, his mercy would have rejoiced and forgiven them. They rejected his overtures but the lesson doesn't have to be lost on us. God wants to be known and fulfill his good plan for us.

God Wants to Be Known

The Apostle Paul prayed *that the God of our Lord Jesus Christ, the Father of glory, may give you the Spirit of wisdom and of revelation in the knowledge of him,* (Ephesians 1:17). And Paul also expresses his own passion: *that I may know him and the power of his resurrection, and may share his sufferings, becoming like him in his death* (Philippians 3:10).

Not only has God revealed himself in the human form of Jesus, which we will address in a few moments, he repeatedly described himself in the Old Testament through the Prophets and his designated leaders like David.

Psalm 103:1-14 reveals a concise description who God really is. I'm going to bold letter the attributes of God which reveal him in truth. God is speaking through David saying, "This is what I'm really like. Anything you believe or have heard different is wrong. I want you to know me in truth and this is the truth." I guess God didn't have to add, "so help me God."

Bless the Lord, O my soul,
and all that is within me,
*bless his **holy** name!*
Bless the Lord, O my soul,
and forget not all his benefits,
*who **forgives** all your iniquity,*
*who **heals** all your diseases,*
*who **redeems** your life from the pit,*
*who **crowns** you with steadfast love and mercy,*
*who **satisfies** you with good*
so that your youth is renewed like the eagle's.
*The Lord **works righteousness***
***and justice** for all who are oppressed.*
*He **made known** his ways to Moses,*
his acts to the people of Israel.
*The Lord is **merciful** and **gracious**,*
***slow to anger** and **abounding in steadfast love**.*
*He will not **always chide**,*
***nor will he keep his anger** forever.*
*He does **not deal** with us according to our sins,*
***nor repay** us according to our iniquities.*
For as high as the heavens are above the earth,
*so great is his **steadfast love** toward those who fear him;*
as far as the east is from the west,
*so far does he **remove our transgressions** from us.*
*As a father shows **compassion** to his children,*
so the Lord shows compassion to those who fear him.
*For he **knows our frame**;*
*he **remembers that we are dust**. (emphasis added)*

Which of those characteristics means the most to you? Which one(s) is hard to believe? Of the one hard to believe, can you think of something in your childhood or adulthood creating doubt about the truth? The answers could be blocking you from being struck with awe at your great God. But don't worry. God knows all that. He was with you and knew how he would work later to correct the lie. Are you willing?

We'll soon see how to identify our wrong perceptions about God. Right now, I'd like to camp on a verse in Psalm 103 we often don't notice. *He made known his ways to Moses, his acts to the people of Israel* (vs. 7).

Before I recognized the importance of verse 7, I didn't think much about the different reactions of Moses and the Israelites. But the differences are remarkable and reveal the two choices we have.

Moses' life was never the same after God revealed himself in a burning bush. From then on, though inadequate and imperfect, he was consumed with bringing glory to God. Moses prayed *Now therefore, if I have found favor in your sight, please show me now your ways, that I may know you in order to find favor in your sight* (Exodus 33:13). Notice his motive? "I want favor through knowing you and your ways." How different from the people Zechariah talked about.

Here's the Amplified version. *Now therefore, I pray you, if I have found favor in Your sight, let me know Your ways so that I may know You [becoming more deeply and intimately acquainted with You, recognizing and understanding Your ways more clearly] and that I may find grace and favor in Your sight.*

Is that your heart's motive and desire, even if imperfectly? If so, God desires to fulfill it. He wants to be known by you. And here's the good news: *And the Lord said to Moses, "This very thing that you have spoken I will do, for you have found favor in my sight, and I know you by name"* (Exodus 33:17).

Let's also look at this verse in the Amplified version. *The Lord said to Moses, "I will also do this thing that you have asked; for you have found favor (lovingkindness, mercy) in My sight and I have known you [personally] by name."*

What did God know about Moses? His heart. His motive. His desire to give God glory. Did Moses always respond perfectly? We know the answer is no. God even prevented him from going into the Promised Land because of Moses' disobedience. But the motives of Moses' heart pleased God.

In contrast to Moses are the Israelites' motives while in the wilderness.

Now when all the people saw the thunder and the flashes of lightning and the sound of the trumpet and the mountain smoking, the people were afraid and trembled, and they stood far off and said to Moses, "You speak to us, and we will listen; but do not let God speak to us, lest we die." Moses said to the people, "Do not fear, for God has come to test you, that the fear of him may be before you, that you may not sin." The people stood far off, while Moses drew near to the thick darkness where God was. Exodus 20:18-21

Moses climbed the mountain with a passion to meet with God and know him better. The Israelites were not only hesitant, they were resistant. They were self-protective. By the time they faced the threat of clouds, smoke, and fire on Mt. Sinai, they have history with God but the knowledge and experience aren't profitable for them. He had delivered them in miraculous ways but they chose to fear instead of trust. Psalm 78:11, 18 explains their motives. *They forgot his works and the wonders that he had shown them. They tested God in their heart by demanding the food they craved.*

The Israelites wanted God to jump through their hoops. To prove himself safe but even when he did, they refused to trust him. Moses clearly states God's motive: *"Fear and trust me so that you will be motivated to not sin thus not suffer the consequences of disobedience. I want the best for you; disobedience isn't it."* Sadly, like the Israelites, if we don't see God's wise and loving motives, we will refuse to trust him.

Predictable God? Not!

One way we become hardened like the Israelites is demanding a predictable and obedient God. If we can know what to expect of him—make him do what we want—we think we'll know him. That's only a selfish strategy to feel secure, not a desire to trust and be in awe of him.

Just ask Allison. Allison's mom would suddenly smack her for seemingly no reason. Her mom would exclaim, "Don't give me that look."

As Allison described this to me, I felt intense sadness. I couldn't imagine not knowing when my mom might suddenly and without any reason smack me. Allison explained, "I'd ask her 'What look, mom?' Kathy, I didn't even realize I was giving any kind of look. Then I would ask her, 'Help me understand what I did so I won't do it again.' She would only reply, 'Don't argue. You know what you're doing.'

"Allison, I can't imagine how that would make you feel. I'm so very sorry."

"Yea, I suppose it was bad; yes, I know it was. Since we've had these sessions together, I see the strategy I formed. I over-explain and over-analyze everything for my daughter. I think I must make logical sense of everything, making it clear to her why I'm doing what I'm doing, so I don't wound her like my mom wounded me.

"And I also have panic attacks if God seems to be doing something different from what I expected. I ask him repeatedly why he's doing something. I want him to be logical. I don't like anything illogical. I see now it reminds me of my mom.

"But God is not my mom. She reacted without wanting my good. I'm learning God's motive is to bring good into my life. He isn't just smacking me. He might be disciplining me but that's out of love for my spiritual growth."

Formulaic God? Not!

In another of our sessions, Allison asked me, "What should I do when my husband says ...?"

I asked, "If I gave you a formula to follow, how would that leave out God?"

At first, she was startled. "I just want to know how to head off a fight. What's so bad about that?"

"I understand that, but how would that leave out God?"

After a few moments, she replied, "Well, I guess I could just depend upon the formula rather than looking to God."

"That's right. You would miss an opportunity to abide. Jesus said he only did what the Father told him to do. Do you think Jesus followed a formula? Was he always predictable?"

These thoughts were almost shocking to Allison. Since then I've begun making a list of the different ways Jesus responded as he abided in the Holy Spirit's power. Wanting to do what his Father wanted him to do brought glory to God. Jesus' varied responses reveal his care, love, and attention to the details of each person's life.

He knows them and is inviting them to know him.

Here are examples from the book of Mark.

Jesus:
invited fishermen to become fishers of men (1:17)
rebuked demons (1:25)
took a sick woman's hand (1:31)
healed the paralytic with a word of forgiveness (2:5)
reasoned with scribes who were reasoning ... within themselves (Mark 2:8)
called Matthew with words Follow me! (2:14)
used parables to touch any receptive hearts (4:9)
hushed a storm (4:39)
allowed healing by a woman touching his hem (5:30)
invited disciples to participate in the provision of food (6:37)
walked on the sea to give peace and courage (6:50)
seemed like he was rejecting a Gentile woman before healing her daughter (7:27)

Additionally, in Luke 5:15-16, he left needy people behind to have a private time with the Father.

But my favorite example is Jesus' sensitive response to the needs of a deaf and dumb man through sign language (Mark 7:31-37). Initially the way Jesus responds to this man seems weird but we couldn't be farther from the truth.

Theologian Sinclair Ferguson comments:

The man could not hear Jesus and he was also incapable of verbal communication. So Jesus "spoke" to him in the language he could understand—sign language. The fingers placed in his ears and then removed meant, 'I am going to remove the blockage in your hearing.' The spitting and the touching of the man's tongue meant, 'I am going to remove the blockage in your mouth.' The glance up to heaven meant, 'It is God alone who is able to do this for you.' Jesus wanted the man to understand that it was not magic but God's grace that healed him.[39]

Jesus doesn't respond with "one size fits all" actions. He chooses what's best for each one.

I would challenge you to make your own study of the different and unique ways God responds throughout the Bible. You'll see his heart of love, grace, and other beautiful attributes. Remember, when you "see" Jesus in the New Testament, you are "seeing" God the Father.

The writer of Hebrews affirms *He is the radiance of the glory of God and the exact imprint of his nature, and he upholds the universe by the word of his power. After making purification for sins, he sat down at the right hand of the Majesty on high* (1:3).

Two Fun Challenges:

Over time I've developed a list of God's attributes by using the alphabet to organize them. Plus, at a woman's retreat when I give a presentation on God's qualities, I use a small group exercise to help the women organize their own list. I first ask them to make small groups of three to five women. Depending on the size of the total group, I assign different parts of the room to take half or a quarter of the alphabet and write down characteristics describing God. Then, I call upon each group to share what they thought. Everyone else writes down the qualities on the handout I supply. I suggest they continue adding to their list after they return home. Invariably the women are shocked, surprised, and thrilled to focus on God's nature. They never realized there were so many characteristics.

I encourage you to make your own list.

Here is Adam Clarke's (1762-1832) description of God. (Quoted in *The Divine Conspiracy* by Dallas Willard)

> God is …
> 'the eternal, independent, and self-existent Being; the Being whose purposes and actions spring from himself, without foreign motive or influence; he who is absolute in dominion; the most pure, the most simple, the most spiritual of all essences; infinitely perfect; and eternally self-sufficient, needing nothing that he has made; illimitable in his immensity, inconceivable in his mode of existence, and indescribable in his essence; known fully only by himself, because an infinite mind can only be fully comprehended by itself. In a word, a Being who, from his infinite wisdom, cannot err or be deceived, and from his infinite goodness, can do nothing but what is eternally just, and right, and kind.'[40]

Another exercise can help reveal how you might be believing lies about God. On the list below prayerfully consider your true honest view of each characteristic that may or may not describe God accurately. There are some qualities which *do not describe* who God really is. Yet we think it's true of him. Or we may not believe it in our minds but our hearts (and actions) respond as if we do. That's the key to uncovering the source of our distrust in God: unearthing what we truly believe and feel about who God is. The more we uncover and then change those lies, the more we'll be in awe to praise him in truth.

Here are the instructions:
Mark "H" beside a quality you feel with your heart.
Mark "M" beside a quality you believe with your mind.
You may mark both or leave blank beside any quality.

loving	omnipotent	omniscient
joyful	(all powerful)	(knows
weak	worried	everything)
determined	trustworthy	impatient
humble	sovereign	forgiving
stingy	changes his mind	keeps track of wrongs
loyal	patient	holy
worthy of praise	reachable	merciful
impartial	angry	just
faithful	creative	fickle
good	majestic	immutable
uncaring	mighty	(never
truthful	omnipresent	changing)
distant	(present	gentle
encouraging	everywhere)	available
self-sufficient	eternal	wrathful
real	unhappy	jealous
wimpy	reliable	changeless
inconsistent in	wise	peaceful
disciplining	steadfast	righteous
immense	generous	unforgiving
present	plays favorites	has poor judgement
glorious	invincible	stable
makes mistakes	beautiful	abusive
great	not worthy of trust	wonderful
excellent	kind	victorious
strong	stubborn	a grudge-holder
	responsive	

After you find the lies you're believing, ask the Holy Spirit to reveal how the lie began. Then you can rebuke the lie each time it resonates in your heart or mind.

You can also find verses in the Bible referring to what is true about God and study those verses to deepen the truth within you. The other side is to research verses proving the opposite of the lies you believe or feel.

That's what Judith did. The second time we met for soul care counseling, she explained what she'd discovered after the first time.

There was a time I believed I was stupid because during my depression while in medical school, I wasn't able to concentrate. I couldn't score an A on a few key tests no matter how hard I studied. Being a perfectionist, getting Bs was not good enough. I told God he made a mistake creating me. I was stupid and a mistake. I told him if he makes no mistakes, then he must not care about me enough to help me. Also, he was not love like it says in the Bible.

After you and I talked, I realized I was saying God doesn't know what he is doing. I also thought he is powerless and a liar. I identified my wound came from being shamed for bad performance growing up and my mom saying she regretted having children. The lies I believed about myself were I'm stupid, a mistake, and unwanted.

Then I could see how those wounds and lies were leading me to believe God was not smart, unwise, incapable, powerless, hopeless, unloving and a liar. I could have told you sincerely I believed all the opposites. But our time together helped me see my sin of cooperating with Satan's whispers.

Now I'm noticing and changing my lies to the truth. He is the source of all knowledge and wisdom. He is capable. He is omnipotent. He is love and he is the truth. So now, I will have to spend some time finding scriptures to support those truths and counteract the lies.

Mary, Mother of Jesus
Luke 1

Put yourself for just a moment into the thinking and feeling of teenaged Mary. Forget we know everything turns out all right. Forget she becomes respected. Forget she has the privilege of birthing and loving the human Son of God. Forget she is protected by God through a godly man who believes the angel.

Forget all that. She was living in the present danger, facing people hating her, misunderstanding her, planning her death. How in the world would you respond to the angel? What would you believe about such a God with a crazy, dangerous plan? The Scriptures she had heard from her parents and other adults her whole life talked about a victorious, conquering King. At least that's what the scribes and Pharisees taught. Certainly not about the Messiah coming as a human baby by a teenaged girl.

No way! Count me out! But we know she didn't say that.

In the sixth month the angel Gabriel was sent from God to a city of Galilee named Nazareth, to a virgin betrothed to a man whose name was Joseph, of the house of David. And the virgin's name was Mary. And he came to her and said, "Greetings, O favored one, the Lord is with you!" But she was greatly troubled at the saying, and tried to discern what sort of greeting this might be. And the angel said to her, "Do not be afraid, Mary, for you have found favor with God. And behold, you will conceive in your womb and bear a son, and you shall call his name Jesus. He will be great and will be called the Son of the Most High. And the Lord God will give to him the throne of his father David, and he will reign over the house of Jacob forever, and of his kingdom there will be no end." Luke 1:26-33

After a few assurances, Mary submits. *And Mary said, "Behold, I am the servant of the Lord; let it be to me according to your word." And the angel departed from her* Luke 1:38.

Mary heads to her cousins' house, Elizabeth and Zechariah. Elizabeth also assures Mary she is carrying the Christ child.

And Mary said,

"My soul magnifies the Lord,
    and my spirit rejoices in God my Savior,
for he has looked on the humble estate of his servant.
    For behold, from now on all generations will call me blessed;
for he who is mighty has done great things for me,
    and holy is his name.
And his mercy is for those who fear him
    from generation to generation.
He has shown strength with his arm;
    he has scattered the proud in the thoughts of their hearts;
he has brought down the mighty from their thrones
    and exalted those of humble estate;
he has filled the hungry with good things,
    and the rich he has sent away empty.
He has helped his servant Israel,
    in remembrance of his mercy,
as he spoke to our fathers,
    to Abraham and to his offspring forever." Luke 1:46-55

That's being struck with awe for God's glory. Use Mary's descriptions of God to add to your list.

Reflection and Discussion Questions

1. What was your first reaction when you saw the title of this chapter? Did your reaction give you any clues as to your attitudes about praising God?

2. What is your current thinking about how or if childhood experiences influence our views of God?

3. Would you share an experience from your childhood that influenced your view of God?

4. J. I. Packer's self-protective sinful strategy was cynicism. Can you identify any of yours?

5. Have you ever tried to influence God for favor based on some form of religiosity? What did that look like and what happened?

6. On a scale from 1 to 10 (10 being fully believe), how much are you convinced God wants to be known by you? How has he revealed he does (or doesn't)?

7. Of God's characteristics named in Psalm 103, which is your favorite?

8. When have you responded like the Israelites in the wilderness?

9. Why do you think we might want a predictable or formulaic God? What are the disadvantages?

10. What lie have you believed about God? How has that prevented you from being struck by awe for God?

11. How does Mary's experience impact you the most?

12. Write down a prayer of praise to Jesus for his work in securing your salvation.

Chapter 9
Steadfast
Exhibit Dependability

The main command the Lord Jesus gives us in order to prevent sin and temptation is to watch. To watch means to be diligent to not be surprised and entangled by temptations. You know that you've fallen into spiritual laziness when you aren't stirred by warnings against sin, when you can't be motivated to spiritual duty, and when you are easily discouraged and give up at the sight of difficulties.[41]—Kris Lundgaard

Patience is the believer's spiritual strength which he has in God whereby he, in the performance of his duty, willingly, with composure, joyfully, and steadfastly endures all the vicissitudes of life, having a hope that the outcome will be well.[42]—Wilhelmus a'Brakel

My cell phone rang; I greeted my neighbor and dear friend, Karen. "Kathy, can you take Stephen and I to the airport tomorrow afternoon?"

"Sure. Would love to."

"Oh, and we're arriving home in three weeks, can you pick us up?" I looked at my calendar and realized Larry and I had tentatively hoped to get away then for a few days. While I hesitated, Karen spoke up, "We can ask someone else so it's no problem if you can't."

A matador could not have waved a redder cape before a bull than those words to this be-dependable-or-die Christian. To say "I can't" would mean causing her to have more trouble and me appearing undependable. After all, helping others is what brings glory to God. Proverbs 12:22 says, *Lying lips are an abomination to the Lord, but those who act faithfully are his delight.*

I knew in my mind I was believing lies, but in my heart, it felt dangerous to say no. My value and worth would be threatened in Karen's eyes. The fact I believed she meant she could find someone else didn't make a difference. How much I valued being seen dependable was in danger along with feeling good about myself—even at the expense of losing time with my husband. How crazy is that?

But crazy motives are often birthed in childhood. That's true for me about my dependability. Remember my earlier story about not wanting to disappoint my favorite teacher, Mrs. Leighton, so I lied to her? My "strategy" became dependability. "If I'm dependable, no one will know the horrible truth that I'm a liar. Dependability is the opposite of lying. If you lie, you don't keep your promises and you aren't dependable. But if you are dependable, no one can call you a liar!" Over many years, I honed the skill of dependability. My teachers described me in every report card with the affirming words, "Kathy is very dependable and conscientious." I made sure no one could ever accuse me of lying.

That's why Karen's request that day brought out the red cape of threatening my dependability. What I thought was a good trait was actually a false worship of my own image.

The Steadfast Pharisees

As you can tell from so many topics in this book, what we call "good" can be motivated by unrighteous goals. One important example in the Bible are the Pharisees who Jesus rebuked in Matthew 23. They are steadfast in obeying God's commands but their objective is the approval and applause of others.

Jesus identifies their heart, what they value (and it's not God's glory):

They do all their deeds to be seen by others (vs 5)
they love the place of honor (vs. 6)
and the best seats in the synagogues (vs. 6)
and greetings in the marketplaces (vs. 7)
being called rabbi by others (vs. 7)

Jesus points out their mixed motives in order to call them to repentance and transformation. He loves them so much he wants them to seek his approval and applause, which is best for them.

Let's look at Jesus' effort to woo them by warning the crowd not to be like the Pharisees. He is saying they look good but their heart isn't motivated by a true love for others. They keep the rules and therefore look dependable but it's empowered by a good self-image. We get the feeling if people didn't respond with admiration they wouldn't be as motivated. In some ways, we might relate more than we'd anticipate so let's see what Jesus says:

Verse 3: you preach but don't practice. Jesus wants our dependability to be motivated by love for others not by having a good image.

Verse 4: you put burdens on others but don't help. Our expectations can be unreasonable. We treat the spiritually weak and new believers as if they should be strong in their faith. We hold up our own steadfastness as an unrealistic goal, which can discourage them.

Verse 5: you promenade showing off your phylacteries and fringes. Phylacteries are boxes containing Scripture verses placed on the foreheads and arms. The longer the fringes, the greater appearance of holiness. Although in the Old Testament God advised these spiritual practices, his motive was to encourage them to remember Scripture not use them for self-promotion. We might quote Scripture or give a testimony seemingly glorifying God but our heart's motive is to lift up ourselves.

Verse 6: you choose places of honor. We may manipulate achieving a coveted position rather than submitting to God's orchestration. We can compare ourselves to others who have "arrived" and make a goal to be like them, not like Jesus.

Verse 7: you love the greetings in marketplaces and being called rabbi. Jesus isn't against any leader or follower being given respect, but the challenge comes when we depend upon people's respect and honor for feeling good about ourselves. God's view of us in Christ isn't of value to us.

Verses 13-15: you train others to be hypocrites like yourselves. When we don't share our own struggles, thus appearing perfectly dependable, we are modeling and training others to being hypocrites like ourselves. Our mentee might think, "My mentor doesn't tell me about her struggles so I shouldn't tell anyone I'm struggling. And she doesn't seem to examine her heart so I guess I don't need to examine mine."

Verses 16-22: you "swear" by (depend upon) the wrong things. We can find our value in our involvement in our church or how often we share Christ.

Verses 23-24: you tithe the smallest thing but ignore God's values. We might be very faithful in giving our tithe, but are critical of those who don't contribute.

Verses 25-28: you focus on appearance not the heart. Our accomplishments become our judge and jury of our worth and value—not God's gracious opinion of us in Christ.

Verses 29-33: you judge those from the past. We might judge a "fallen" Christian leader by saying we would never do the same thing.

Verse 31-39: you disregard God's provision of loving correction. When God leads someone to offer us correction, we might point out some fault in their life.

We've all stumbled in some manner along the lines of Jesus' comments and it would be easy to feel overwhelmed, even condemned. But that is not God's heart, nor mine. He offers forgiveness, redemption, help, and support. He doesn't condemn us nor heap contempt upon us. Romans 5:1 assures us there is no condemnation in Christ. But in order to make changes in our lives and bring God glory, we must first identify what's muddy in our motives. I can understand if it seems Jesus' words are harsh. Jesus knew strong words were the only thing that might pull them out of their steadfast determination to reject God and misuse his principles. The Pharisees were convinced their faithfulness to rules, legalism, and commands were righteous. But they were living under a burden Jesus pointed out because he knows it isn't good for them.

The Holy Spirit's call to us to abandon our sinful steadfastness is the same loving effort. Trying to please others, keep rules, be perfect, never make a mistake, and whatever other ways we are defining dependability, faithfulness, or steadfastness only serve to burden us. We're not trusting God and resting in his grace.

Larry and I refer to the metaphor of "holding up the Titanic." Not only are we trying to hold up the Titanic by being steadfast (or any other misused "good" thing), we are arranging the deck chairs on a sinking ship. Jesus offers something else.

> Come to me, all who labor and are heavy laden, and I will give you rest. Take my yoke upon you, and learn from me, for I am gentle and lowly in heart, and you will find rest for your souls. For my yoke is easy, and my burden is light. Matthew 11:28-30

Only if our steadfastness is stimulated by trust in God are we taking on his yoke. If our actions stem from fear about being misunderstood, the opinions of others, or believing God can't bring good from our mistakes or problems, we are heaving a heavy yoke onto our shoulders.

That is true of a woman I met at a women's retreat I'll call Adrian. She told me of teaching her friends sexual acts at age twelve. She was being sexually abused herself. She knows now her victimization was not her fault but she still feels horrible about abusing other children.

As a result, she is a "helicopter" mother, terrified of any potential danger, and furious with her husband who doesn't supervise their children like she does. She receives praise from other moms for her faithful and involved mothering. But after hearing me speak, she recognized her motive was paying penance by protecting her children from harm. If successful, she could be cleansed from her abuse of other children. She felt desperate to protect her children from someone like herself.

My heart hurt for her. She expressed relief in sharing with me and we spent some time in prayer, including her asking God's forgiveness. We've kept in touch. God has continued her healing process and she is learning to put down the Titanic and take up Jesus' easy yoke.

Ready to Fast?

Before you stop reading because you don't want to go without food, let me explain the kind of spiritual discipline I'm suggesting. Its goal is to loosen the power of a mixed motive. If you've been wondering, "How can I tell if a choice is pure or not? How can I tell if my tendency to want to appear steadfast (or anything else that might be wrongly motivated) is for God's glory or my glory?"

This kind of fast is what the psalmist David writes in Psalm 139:23-24.

> Search me, O God, and know my heart!
> Try me and know my thoughts!
> And see if there be any grievous way in me,
> and lead me in the way everlasting!

One way to allow God to search our hearts for "grievous ways" is to think of God calling you to do the opposite of what you value about yourself. Or what you find pride in. Or what you demand you must have.

Haven't we all said something like (or thought it), "I take pride in my dependability, honesty, trust in God, love for others, or any other good thing"? Pick whichever one is applicable to you. Then be honestly aware of what your heart is feeling and prompting while thinking, "What would my reaction be if God asked me to make a conscious choice to not be dependable ... etc.?"

Do you feel tense? Do you feel irritated? Do you feel resistant?

Right about now, you could be thinking, "Well, God would never invite me to not do something good. He wants me to always do good." I understand your thinking.

At this point of evaluation, I want to stress I'm not saying you should follow up on doing it. I'm only saying get in touch with what it reveals within your heart by your feelings. If there's resistance of any kind (tension, irritation, or anything different than surrender), there's a possibility the "good response" is more about your glory than God's glory. If something is for God's glory, we'll be willing to do whatever God wants, even if we don't understand his reasoning.

Certainly, all our motives are mixed to some degree. Remember, we'll never become perfectly unmixed. There will always be a certain level of muddiness. But because God loves us and knows what's best for us, he invites us to become more purified all the time. That's called sanctification. God asks us to look into the mirror evaluating our reflection (James 1:23-24). Our initial feelings can indicate our heart's motives so we don't walk away from that mirror deceived.

Here's an example of God's fast for me, which was his invitation to be relieved of a heavy yoke of sinful steadfastness.

From the beginning of my ministry in 1980, I had always prided myself on responding to every letter and phone call (in the early days), and later with the advance of technology, every email or comment on social media because a dependable person does. I felt tense when I didn't. What would someone think? I don't care about them? I'm rejecting them? (By the way did you notice the indication of a murky motive? Pride. Pride is totally about my image not God's glory.)

When God called Larry and I to a sabbatical from ministry eleven years ago, I had been sending out a weekly email to over a thousand contacts with what I called "From One Princess to Another," which contained a quote, scripture verse, and insight. Very short but women loved it. And whenever anyone wrote back, I always replied with warm appreciation.

As a part of our sabbatical, I sent one last email explaining why

I wouldn't be sending out the emails. As I pushed "send," I could identify in my soul something akin to a dog being thirsty and seeing a dish of water. I eagerly awaited the reply emails and I was not disappointed. Women responded saying how much they loved my emails and how much they would miss them. The replies of love and appreciation were powerful … and they hydrated my soul.

As Larry saw what was happening, he said, "I think I should open these emails and reply for you. I think you are gaining too much value from them, diverting your attention from your value in Christ."

As he said these words, my chest tightened and I felt irritated. How dare he point out my muddy and mixed motives? How dare he suggest removing my fix for appreciation and adoration? What could be wrong with replying and making the women feel good?

Plus, I considered the kind of reply Larry would give and I felt panicky. He would be using my email address and the women wouldn't know he was replying—not me. I knew how he would reply. With two words: "Thank you." Where's the warmth in that? Where's the encouragement for others? Where's my appearance of steadfast caring? No. where.

This was occurring after we had been confronted with our mixed and murky motives at a seminar for learning soul-care counseling for others and ourselves through the ministry of Journey Companions Ministries (www.JourneyCompanionsMinistries.org). A verse which had become instructional and inspirational to us from the teaching was Jeremiah 2:13.

> for my people have committed two evils:
> they have forsaken me,
> the fountain of living waters,
> and hewed out cisterns for themselves,
> broken cisterns that can hold no water.

As Larry suggested me "fasting" from seeing and replying to the emails, Jeremiah 2:13 convicted me. Like a panting thirsty dog, I was running quickly to the dirty cistern and drinking muddy water. The water seemed pure but was not because it wasn't from God's fountain of living waters.

With some resistance, I agreed with Larry. He began to open those emails, and I didn't read the greetings. He replied with two words, "Thank you." I was deprived of the applause and approval I knew those emails contained. I recognized my fear of what the women would think. I could feel the stronghold of my idol of dependability trying with all its might to hold on with its tentacles around my heart.

The "fast" loosened those tentacles. I ran panting more often to God's living spring to gain my approval, applause, and appreciation from his view of me in Christ.

Remember my opening story in this chapter of being "dependable" by offering to pick up my friends from the airport—even at the cost of missing time away with Larry (which I initiated, by the way)? The next day when I was ready to take them to the airport, Karen called saying their plane had been delayed. I knew this was my opportunity to "fast" from my need to appear steadfast.

"Karen, I let my idol of dependability convince me to say yes to picking you up. Larry and I actually are hoping to get out of town during that time. I hate to inconvenience you but can you find someone else?"

Karen quickly said, "No problem, because our friend at church wanted to drive us but we said we had someone already. I'll let him know he's on. No problem."

God had provided. I was so glad and even more grateful for God's empowering to loosen my muddy motive.

Martha
Luke 10:38-42

I wonder if Martha, the sister of Mary, was the dependability queen in her town, Bethany. I can just imagine at the Women of the Temple Committee meeting for the upcoming women's luncheon event, the chairperson asking, "Now who can we get to cater the lunch?"

Everyone looks around and another woman asks, "Where's Martha?"

Mary speaks up, "Oh, she's at the meeting for the Temple Benevolence committee."

A third woman raises her hand. After being called on by the chairperson, Lydia says, "Ask Martha. She'll do it."

Could Martha have worn an invisible S on her tunic? No, not for Superman, although many most likely called her Superwoman. But S for steadfast and its twin sister, dependability. Why else would Martha have been so crazy busy when Jesus came visiting? Remember the story?

> Now as they went on their way, Jesus entered a village. And a woman named Martha welcomed him into her house. And she had a sister called Mary, who sat at the Lord's feet and listened to his teaching. But Martha was distracted with much serving. And she went up to him and said, "Lord, do you not care that my sister has left me to serve alone? Tell her then to help me." But the Lord answered her, "Martha, Martha, you are anxious and troubled about many things, but one thing is necessary. Mary has chosen the good portion, which will not be taken away from her."
> Luke 10:38-42

What motivated Martha? Of course we'll never know conclusively her heart's motive. But as women, so many of us are like her because we have chosen the same technique to gain approval and applause: busyness and productivity. We know Martha didn't have to do everything she did because Mary, who was equally considered the hostess, didn't. I have no doubt Mary did what she was supposed to do and then chose to abide at Jesus' feet. If Martha is like me, she thought of "one more thing," "one more dish," "one more decorating touch," "one more ..." Did she think, "Just wait until Jesus sees this. He'll feel so important and valued." I would have.

But Jesus loves Martha's soul *well*. He doesn't want her to carry the heavy yoke she puts upon her own shoulders and the muddy cistern she is gulping from. He doesn't need anything to make him feel important or valuable. He only seeks his Father's approval and applause.

In his concern for her he woos her by pointing out the result of her sin: anxiety, anger, critical spirit, feeling abandoned, even blaming Jesus for not making Mary do what Martha thought she should do. She accused Jesus of not caring for her. Most importantly, her motive was to provide rather than abide. Jesus was saying, "I love you too much. Please look at what you're doing and why you're doing it. Come and abide."

He says the same things to us.

Reflection and Discussion Questions

1. Do you think of yourself as very steadfast or dependable? Explain. How did you feel reading this chapter?

2. If you consider yourself not driven by a wrong motive for dependability, to what do you credit that?

3. Can you think of and share a time when you agreed to something in order to be seen as dependable or faithful but you knew it wasn't God's will? What happened as a result?

4. Are you a person who has a difficult time saying no? Explain why or why not.

5. How do you feel reading about Jesus' critique of the Pharisees in Matthew 23?

6. Can you identify with any of the Pharisees' attitudes and behavior Jesus identifies in Matthew 23? How do you handle the temptation to feel discouraged, condemned, or discouraged?

7. Does "holding up the Titanic" apply to your life? If so, explain or describe one example. How does Matthew 11:28-30 speak to you?

8. Is God calling you to "fast" about something in order to loosen the mixed motives of ungodly steadfastness or dependability—or any disordered action?

9. Can you identify any way you are drinking muddy spiritual water from a cistern in your heart? What do you think God wants you to do about it?

10. Think of something you do "for the Lord and his glory" and ask the Holy Spirit to enlighten your motive for doing it. Make a list of both godly motivations and ungodly motivations in that choice.

11. Did you have any different or new insight about Martha? To what degree do you relate to her?

12. Is it possible Mary had her own kind of "dependability" cistern in sitting at Jesus' feet? Explain.

Chapter 10
Sensitive
Share God's Design

Think of emotions as a language. They say something—something very important—and part of our job is to figure out what they are saying.[43]—Ed Welch

Silence frees us from the need to control others. One reason we can hardly bear to remain silent is that it makes us feel so helpless. We are accustomed to relying upon words to manage and control others. A frantic stream of words flows from us in an attempt to straighten others out. We want so desperately for them to agree with us, to see things our way … We devour people with our words.[44]—Richard Foster

I had a sinking feeling in the pit of my stomach when we concluded our phone conversation. Even though I'd had the opportunity to tell my friend about the gospel, I was crushed to think of the way I'd done it. *Why didn't I ask more questions instead of preaching? Why didn't I inquire about her beliefs about God? Did I communicate condemnation or hope?* I tried to remember what had been said. I couldn't remember much but it felt like I'd done more wrong things than good. After all, she didn't repent and receive Christ.

As I continued to rehearse the conversation, I prayed, *Oh, Lord, somehow use for good all my inadequacies. I know you love her but since I'm representing you, I want to represent you well.*

I wanted to believe the truth another person's response wasn't up to me, but Satan's flaming missiles hurtling toward my mind and heart seemed so convincing. They seemed like truth because

"I'm stupid."

"I talked too much."

"I didn't interpret her words correctly."

"If she doesn't come to know Christ, it's all my fault."

As I thought later about why I persist in being tempted by such lies, I realized my motive. If I share correctly and gain the results I want, I can boast of how God used me. I'll look wise and obedient to the Spirit. But focusing so much on me actually hampers my ability to listen to the Holy Spirit's prompting so that I can be sensitive to the needs of the other person.

It's like a whirlwind of conflicting thoughts and emotions. It feels overwhelming. And overall, whether I'm trying to encourage another believer or share the gospel with unbelievers, I'm tempted to think I must do it right (my definition of right) otherwise all is lost and God can't be glorified. But I'm learning to relax and trust him. My mixed motives are becoming more purified. The same can be for you.

God Is in Charge of His Glory

One major way I'm learning to trust him more is believing even my mistakes are useable by God for his glory. I'm not responsible for the growth of a believer or the salvation of an unbeliever.

The Apostle Paul has the godly perspective. *But with me it is a very small thing that I should be judged by you or by any human court. In fact, I do not even judge myself. For I am not aware of anything against myself, but I am not thereby acquitted. It is the Lord who judges me* (I Corinthians 4:3-4).

Paul doesn't jump into self-contempt like I do. He seeks God's opinion. I think so many of us depend upon our self-evaluations rather than looking to God for his judgement of what happened. We conclude we didn't say the right things. But we don't know what our friend needed to hear. Maybe the very words we said—and are judging—were what she needed to hear.

So many times I've followed up on a conversation, like yesterday, and apologized for what I said. Most of the time—like yesterday—the other person replied, "Really? I don't remember." Or another time, a friend said, "No, I didn't think anything bad." I had been all upset, rehearsing what I said, but my friend wasn't.

Paul continues, *We are fools for Christ's sake, but you are wise in Christ. We are weak, but you are strong. You are held in honor, but we in disrepute* (vs. 10).

Evidently Paul's opponents in Corinth are saying those things about him, so he is responding sarcastically. He's basically saying, "Of course, you're right. You are wise but we are fools. You are strong but we are weak. You are held in honor but we are disreputable. Shame on us."

He is making light of their opinions of him because he doesn't mind being seen in those ways. His motive is not to be seen well but to cooperate with God's plan. What a lesson for us. We don't have to mind what others say either.

If we are afraid of appearing as fools when we speak of the Lord, we might want to examine our hearts. We could evaluate whether our self-contempt is because we fear looking foolish or silly or unintelligent or whatever we have vowed to never appear as or feel like. When we have the purified heart of sacrifice for God's glory, we will be wisely sensitive to the needs of others, led by the Holy Spirit, because our focus isn't distracted by our own self-protection.

I have recognized my distracted focus of not wanting to seem stupid or insensitive. Both prevent me from boldly obeying the Spirit's leading. I'm afraid my stupidity will be revealed by saying something someone can dispute from Scripture or their own interpretation of truth. My old nemesis from childhood—don't make anyone feel bad because then I'm bad—hampers me from having the freedom to respond however the Holy Spirit is leading me.

Yet, what is the truth? Paul states the truth earlier in this first letter to the Corinthians, *But we have the mind of Christ* (2:16).

The Corinthian believers must really be struggling with their image. Paul confronts those issues in so many ways. He also writes, *For I decided to know nothing among you except Jesus Christ and him crucified. And I was with you in weakness and in fear and much trembling, and my speech and my message were not in plausible words of wisdom, but in demonstration of the Spirit and of power, so that your faith might not rest in the wisdom of men but in the power of God* (I Corinthians 2:2-5).

Paul seems to be saying, "I have known the fears of appearing weak and lacking wisdom just like you are experiencing. But my weaknesses mean you'll rest in God's power and not depend upon me being so wise."

To some degree I've seen God newly empower my life with a bold sensitivity by being willing to sacrifice my own image or risk being misunderstood.

In the opening story for this chapter, I shared my self-contempt rehearsing all the wrong responses I'd given to my unbelieving friend. But then God popped a great thought into my mind. "Well, if she becomes a Christian, it *certainly* won't be because of my communication skills."

Then, the truth hit me. If her conversion is not because of me, who is the cause? And who will get the glory since I don't deserve it? Jesus and his Spirit. If I had been brilliant and my friend suddenly exclaimed, "Oh, you've made it so clear. I do want to become a Christian," it would have been easy to give myself credit rather than the work of the Holy Spirit. But he is the one who calls her to salvation, it's not about me at all. I'm just a weak and inadequate vessel.

Having purer motives for God's glory doesn't mean we don't prepare as much as we can. Let's talk about ways we can reach out to others with a sensitive spirit, not just sharing the message of salvation but ministering to the needs of others as well.

Are We "Miserable Comforters"?

The book of Job gives us wisdom and direction. Job has been hit by everything that could possibly go bad in a person's life. All his children are killed. All his possessions are destroyed. His wife tells him to forsake God and kill himself. His body is ravaged by disease. And then his friends arrive. Here's the story.

Now when Job's three friends heard of all this evil that had come upon him, they came each from his own place, Eliphaz the

Temanite, Bildad the Shuhite, and Zophar the Naamathite. They made an appointment together to come to show him sympathy and comfort him. And when they saw him from a distance, they did not recognize him. And they raised their voices and wept, and they tore their robes and sprinkled dust on their heads toward heaven. And they sat with him on the ground seven days and seven nights, and no one spoke a word to him, for they saw that his suffering was very great. Job 2:11-13

Their motives are wonderful. They hear of his pain and make specific plans to come show him "sympathy and comfort." They cry at the sight of him. They tear their robes in grief. They sit with him for seven days in silence. They feel Job's physical, emotional, and spiritual pain. There's no judgment or pat answers. They are there for him exactly the way he needs.

But then things change. They start talking and putting their feet in their mouths. Their motive seems to be to solve Job's problem, tell him their version of the truth, and most of all, get him to repent of his sin. Yet Job maintains his innocence during their tirades.

Job's reaction? *I have heard many such things; miserable comforters are you all* (16:2).

What did these "miserable comforters" or "sorry counselors" (NASB) do? Let's review some of them and see what we can learn not to do.

Make broad statements not taking into account Job's faithful life. Eliphaz gives the impression the innocent do not suffer. Therefore, Job must be guilty of something. Eliphaz says, *Remember: who that was innocent ever perished? Or where were the upright cut off?* (4:7).

Make assumptions. Eliphaz also says, *As I have seen, those who plow iniquity and sow trouble reap the same* (4:8). In other words,

"Job, since you have troubles, you created them through your former choices."

The hard thing to understand in all these conversations is some of the comments are true. For instance, we often do reap what we sow. But Job's friends show no compassion or sensitivity in his time of need. And Eliphaz doesn't inquire as to the details of what happened. He never asked something like, "Are there any ways these circumstances could be because of the choices you made?" The friends only state pat answers based on assumptions about Job's circumstances. We need to be careful not to do the same thing.

Tell, but not ask. Job tries to defend himself but Eliphaz and Job's friends aren't really listening to hear Job's heart. They might hear his words but they aren't comprehending because their pre-conceived views block understanding. If they'd really wanted to know Job's heart, they would have found out he had a tremendous passion for God.

One important response of sensitivity are questions like, "Tell me in other words what you're saying because I'm not sure I understand." "How do you define that word you're using? When I use that word, I define it this way. Is that what you mean?"

Pre-determine guilt. Another friend, Bildad, tells him (and can't you just hear his haughty tone of voice?), *Ask the former generations and find out what their fathers learned, for we were born only yesterday and know nothing, and our days on earth are but a shadow. Will they not instruct you and tell you? Will they not bring forth words from their understanding?* (8:8-10).

You can hear Bildad's contempt and disdain. He doesn't want to hear any of Job's grieving feelings or doubts. He doesn't want to examine Job's claims of being righteous. Today some Christians say we shouldn't express a struggling faith. "Just think positively. Don't express doubt." Actually, Jesus responded graciously to the father who said, *I believe; help my unbelief* (Mark 9:24). God honors honesty. He knows our feelings and thoughts anyway.

Give pat answers and easy solutions. Zophar says in Job 11:13-17

If you prepare your heart,
you will stretch out your hands toward him.
If iniquity is in your hand, put it far away,
and let not injustice dwell in your tents.
Surely then you will lift up your face without blemish;
you will be secure and will not fear.
You will forget your misery;
you will remember it as waters that have passed away.
And your life will be brighter than the noonday;
its darkness will be like the morning.

Do you perceive the subtle "If only..."? "If only you'll prepare your heart ... then things will go well." That's one of the characteristics of a "miserable comforter." Such comments are rarely helpful. Most of the time there is no guarantee of a fast solution.

Require complete agreement. Bildad says, *When will you end these speeches? Be sensible, and then we can talk. Why are we regarded as cattle and considered stupid in your sight?* (18:2-3). What he's really saying is, "Accept everything we say without argument or discernment. We know what's best for you." He "plays" God—telling Job everything he should be doing.

What drives Bildad to respond like that? Bildad is defensive because he has interpreted Job's comments as saying, "You don't know anything. I'm smarter than you." Even if Job is saying that (and in some ways he is), Bildad believes his own worth and value are defined by Job. Bildad isn't looking to Jehovah for his value and worth fearing he is indeed unintelligent. Bildad wants to hear how smart he is from Job.

You and I can easily become defensive, even angry, if the person we're helping doesn't jump on our bandwagon. We will feel threatened if we are looking for him to agree with us and therefore affirm our intelligence, wisdom, or whatever it is we value in ourselves. We are completely leaving out God's value of us "in Christ." Only when we sacrifice our own image with the goal of seeing God's wisdom magnified can we bring glory to God.

Be motivated by being ignored. All along, a man named Elihu has been listening to Job and his friends. Finally, he can't stand it anymore and gives his two cents worth. He bursts out, *I also will declare my opinion. For I am full of words; the spirit within me constrains me* (32:17-18). If Elihu had stayed quiet, he most likely would have been considered the wisest of them all. But he can't stand being ignored or not offering his wisdom. Notice the spirit compelling Elihu. It's not the loving Spirit of God. It's his own inner drive to declare his wisdom.

I confess it's hard for me to stay quiet. Feeling ignored makes me feel … *stupid.* If I don't say anything, it means I'm not smart enough to have an opinion. It feels like I'm voiceless. And that means I'm … *stupid.* Oh, how this web of lies wraps its sticky threads around me.

But after giving many hours of soul care, I recognize the value of not saying anything if the Holy Spirit leads. Many times, hurting people need a quiet counselor to be able to work through what God is saying to them in their hearts. By truly listening without trying to form my next bit of "wisdom," I earn the right to ask questions and interact at a deeper level. I will usually take notes because then I don't feel compelled to speak up right away afraid I'll forget my brilliant thought. I can relax and truly listen, asking God to help me know the person's heart.

I wish Job's friends had given him some support and true "comfort." In the end, Almighty God rebuked those friends and ministered to Job. Not in the way we might expect. God actually confronted Job and Job responded:

> Then Job answered the Lord and said:
> "I know that you can do all things,
> and that no purpose of yours can be thwarted.
> 'Who is this that hides counsel without knowledge?'
> Therefore I have uttered what I did not understand,
> things too wonderful for me, which I did not know.
> 'Hear, and I will speak;
> I will question you, and you make it known to me.'
> I had heard of you by the hearing of the ear,
> but now my eye sees you;
> therefore I despise myself,
> and repent in dust and ashes." Job 42:1-6

Although we all would like to hear similar words from the person we're ministering to, the result is always up to God. And even when there doesn't seem to be a preferred response, we can be confident in God's ability to persevere because of his love for them.

God did provide human comfort for Job. Here's the end of the story:

> And the Lord restored the fortunes of Job, when he had prayed for his friends. And the Lord gave Job twice as much as he had before. Then came to him all his brothers and sisters and all who had known him before, and ate bread with him in his house. And they showed him sympathy and comforted him for all the evil that the Lord had brought upon him. And each of them gave him a piece of money and a ring of gold. Job 42:10-11

In all the years I've studied the book of Job, I never paid attention to the fact Job's brothers and sisters and those who *had known him before* came to minister to him. They gave him what he needed all along: sympathy and comfort. Plus, a piece of money and a ring of gold to restore what his calamities had stolen from him.

As for the mention of "the evil" God put upon him? Well, that's the subject for another time and book.

What Does "Sensitivity" Look Like?

As our hearts grow more purified through God's work, we will be able to set aside our own issues, images, and demands to be seen a certain way more and more. It's always a learning process.

Here are some ideas for guiding us along the way.

1. Help the hurting person find the underlying cause of her reactions. Often, she is focusing upon what seems to be the obvious, current reason for her pain.

For instance, "If only my husband would stop working so much, I could be content." The fact is her contentment doesn't need to be based upon the way her husband treats her. She is believing the lie his lack of attention reflects her unworthiness of love. She agrees with Satan's arrow and blames her husband for her discontent. As you can now imagine, some wound from her childhood including teen age years are most likely the source of this lie.

Many people discount the power past painful experiences have upon them now. But those hurtful experiences built a foundation of distrust in God that can influence our reactions and motives now. Even if we've gone through spiritual heart healing, quite often God wants to do a deeper level of healing. Like peeling an onion, he knows there's still vestiges affecting us.

I'll never forget talking with a woman who was very angry with her husband because he wouldn't attend their daughter's drill team performances. I asked her about her childhood and amongst other things she said, "My father never came to watch me perform with the marching band." She saw the connection and realized because she'd never forgiven her father, she was overreacting to her husband's responses. In tears, she said she wanted to forgive both of them.

In Chapter 7, I offered some questions for cross-examining ourselves to determine our motives. We can use the same kinds of questions when addressing others. Here's how those questions can be re-worded. And remember these are not in any kind of order. Use a particular question as the Holy Spirit leads.

- What is the most hurtful thing anyone has ever said or done to you?

- Do you have anything selfish to gain from this choice?

- What do you want to avoid being seen as/like?

- How do you want to be seen?

- What does her reaction or behavior seem to say about you?

- What step of surrender is God inviting you into by allowing these circumstances?

- What would you really like to say to that person and what does it indicate about what you hope to gain?

- What do you hope to gain from disobeying God?

- What does believing that lie protect you from?

- How does this situation or that person's response remind you of your childhood?

- If you obey God, what desire will you not receive?

- Why does your desire seem so important?

- What do you think you deserve? If you don't receive it, what does it seem to say about your worth and value?

- You may be thinking you need to do that, but did God ask you to?

- How do you want to respond that is similar to the way you responded as a child?

- If you obey God, what might he want to accomplish in you, for others, or for his glory?

- If you disobey God, what might be the consequences?

- What does your (godly or ungodly) desire say about who God is?

- Do you feel like God is treating you like that dangerous person did during your childhood?

- What does this possible choice really say about who God is and how he works?

Most often, asking questions are far more impactful than telling someone only what to do. When there is a heart change in her motives, there are ripples into her behavior for more than the "problem" she came to discuss.

2. Reflect back and help her explore her feelings. Romans 12:15 tells us, *Rejoice with those who rejoice, weep with those who weep.* Say things like, "I can really hear the hurt in your voice" or "You must really be feeling angry about that." The best comment is, "Tell me more about that." A powerful question is, "When did you experience this same feeling in your childhood?"

Quite often we feel reluctant to reflect their feeling, especially an "ungodly" one, because it'll seem like we are putting a stamp of approval upon it. But understanding their feeling is the pathway to discovering the underlying cause.

3. Express realistic expectations of growth or healing. Paul was realistic in his letter to his friends in Philippi. *And I am sure of this, that he who began a good work in you will bring it to completion at the day of Jesus Christ* (Philippians 1:6). When is that "completion" day? When a person dies or Jesus returns. Paul is acknowledging his friends will always be experiencing God's "work" of purification of their motives.

Don't promise instant deliverance or fast growth. Healing and growth take time, but she will grow closer to God as she works through the struggle. One of the most important Biblical concepts

I speak about when addressing perfectionism is the "One Percent Principle." I teach others to make small steps of growth, even 1%, rather than 100% goals, which are impossible to meet and create a sense of failure.

Resist giving advice but ask a question like, "What is God inviting you to do?" Although what she senses might be what God wants, she might frame it in an "all or nothing" expectation. She may say, "I think God wants me to always treat my husband with respect." Such words indicate an unrealistic expectation. God works most often through progress not perfection, as we discussed in Chapter 5. Give her the perfectionism quiz I included there. You may find more perfectionist expectations within her than she realizes.

4. Help in practical ways as God leads. Romans 12:13 tells us, *Contribute to the needs of the saints and seek to show hospitality.* If a woman needs specific help, assist her or direct her to someone who can give her aid. Sometimes your needy friend doesn't have the emotional strength to follow through. Making a few phone calls on her behalf may be the difference between success and failure.

The challenge for our motives is following what God wants us to do. An opportunity to help another isn't necessarily God's open door for us. If we help because of wanting to look good or feeling obligated, we aren't honoring the Lord. We may even be preventing God from involving who he wants to assist because we're stepping into the shoes he wanted them to fill.

Galatians 6:2, 5 gives us some guidelines. *Bear one another's burdens, and so fulfill the law of Christ. For each will have to bear his own load.*

The two commands almost seem contradictory. We're supposed to bear one another's burdens but let others bear their own load? Doesn't make sense.

But notice the different words. With some people they are burdened. With others they are carrying a load. I wonder if we can define a "burden" as beyond what the person is currently capable of "bearing." An abused wife who is convinced by her husband their marriage's problems are all her fault will most likely not have the emotional strength to look into a woman's shelter. She may be convinced her life would be threatened if she takes any action. Plus, she may not have the privacy to make phone calls or even look for places to move. We will need to help her in tangible ways to take action.

On the other hand, a person who is strong enough to bear their own load is capable. They may not be choosing to take an action but they could. Of course, it takes God's wisdom to know the difference between these two. God can lead us. But we may not be able to sense his leading if our compulsion to help for wrong reasons is blocking us. And of course, seeking the wisdom of others is always an option.

5. Don't grow weary. Hebrews 12:3 encourages us: *Consider him who endured from sinners such hostility against himself, so that you may not grow weary or fainthearted.* Helping others isn't always easy or fast. Growth might take a long time. Communicate generously to her you aren't impatiently waiting for her to become perfect. And call upon God's strength to persevere. The writer of Hebrews says knowing how Jesus endured and persevered in the midst of great hostility can inspire us.

There will be times when you think God's Spirit has made a breakthrough. But it may not be permanent. There still may be ups and downs. But isn't that true of my life and yours? Just look at Peter who became a strong disciple. Jesus didn't give up on him when he kept opening his mouth and saying something foolish. Jesus had confidence in the Spirit's strength to work in Peter's life (and all followers Jesus left behind) so Jesus could leave for heaven.

If you do become weary, you may be tempted to say things like, "You did it again!" or "What did I tell you last week?" If you're about to express frustration, pay attention to your heart's motives. You may think your friend's success or growth is a reflection of you and your abilities. Or your motive is to have her praise you for your great work in her life. You aren't anyone's Holy Spirit and he's the only one making any changes. You are his vessel, yes, but you are only a conduit. God can use anyone. Give God the glory.

6. Pray with them. Philippians 1:4 is only one of many expressions of what Paul prayed: *always in every prayer of mine for you all making my prayer with joy.* He told them what he was praying for them for their encouragement and instruction.

Not only should you pray for her but in her presence, let her hear your prayer on her behalf. It's often effective to pray something like, "Heavenly Father, Susie is really feeling depressed and desperate right now ..." Bringing her pain before God's throne will comfort and affirm her.

Resist preaching to her or telling her what to do through the means of prayer. And of course, pray as the Holy Spirit leads.

7. Say too little rather than too much. James 1:19 tells us, *Know this, my beloved brothers: let every person be quick to hear, slow to speak, slow to anger.*

Sometimes your silence is more supportive than lots of words. I remember a time when a woman shared a deep sin and I was speechless. Later, she told me my silence was encouraging and helped her move out of her bondage. I'd thought I'd been a failure to not have the right words, but God knew what she needed.

Do all these ideas seem overwhelming? Let me assure you none of us remember or are motivated to follow them all the time. It's a growing process for each of us along with the woman we are helping. Our confidence must be in God wanting to use us for his glory, knowing he can cover our mistakes. We can take confidence and comfort in the truth of Hebrews 12:12: *Therefore lift your drooping hands and strengthen your weak knees.* God wouldn't tell us to do something unless he knows his plan for it.

Our confidence in him helps to purify our motives because we don't have to be tense to make sure something happens the way we think it should.

I had that confidence tested just this week. A friend, Jacqueline, wrote in an email, "Please pray for me to have clarity about how to prevent another major disaster with my father. I need to find a facility that will help him if he falls again. I'm feeling anxious about knowing of a good place for him to rehab if he breaks something again. The last place was horrible and I'm determined not to be blindsided again."

I heard Jacqueline's cry because I have taken care of two elderly parents, my mother and my mother-in-law. Finding good health care can be daunting. But as I felt her pain, I saw several red flags possibly pointing to distrusting God. She was demanding she not be blindsided. And she was feeling anxious. Both of those could be motivating her desperate search. I wondered how she felt about herself when she was "blindsided" before? Did she feel inadequate? Did she judge herself an unloving daughter? What was her motive in judging herself as blindsided? Was she believing God had not sovereignly allowed the difficulty?

I didn't know Jacqueline really well but I knew she was a strong Christian who wanted to trust God. So I prayed, wondering if God wanted me to address what I "heard." I wrote back to her, "As for your dad, I can understand your tension. I will be praying for clarity. And yet, can I be so bold to suggest the Lord may not give you a plan that prevents you being blindsided? I'm learning more and more to yes, plan, but then abide. Walk with him even in the uncertainty.

Yes, I'm sure research is necessary. But if my heart is demanding I prevent something, then usually my heart isn't trusting him. Then my motive is to prevent pain yet God may even want the pain for my growth."

After I clicked on Send I began to doubt. *Was that really God's leading? What did my words convey? How is she receiving it? I should have called her or asked if I could share with her what I was perceiving. I should email her again and apologize.*

Yet in the end I decided to trust God with my fears and trust him to empower me for whatever happened. I recognized my heart's strategy to avoid misunderstanding by second-guessing God's leading. I wanted to make sure I was seen a certain way. Crazy though it was, I was doing the same thing she was: determining how to stay out of pain. I decided I wouldn't follow through and instead "fast" from trying to clear things up for my assurance. If God led me later to contact her, I would obey.

For the next two days with no reply from Jacqueline, I wondered how she was doing and what her reaction was. I prayed for her. Then I saw an email from her in my inbox. With trepidation, I opened it. She wrote, "Thank you so very much, Kathy, for your kind words of admonition, a perfect blend of truth and grace I definitely needed to hear! I appreciate you so much. You have truly been an answer to prayer!"

Even though the results were wonderful, I don't have perfect confidence my response was God's leading. Looking back, I can see the wiser choice would have been to ask if I could call her. That way she could have an opportunity to dialog and clarify her words. Or flat out tell me I was misinterpreting her words. Emails aren't the best way to inquire into a person's heart motives.

But God was gracious and used for his glory my inadequacy. And I'm confident he will do the same for you—for his glory.

Priscilla and Aquila
Acts 18:24-28

Have you ever been in a situation where you recognized a person needed correction? Or maybe someone has come to you with great emotional hurts or is facing something fearful? In the case of Priscilla and Aquila, they heard the teaching of a gifted "preacher" who didn't quite have all the facts. Here's the story.

> Now a Jew named Apollos, a native of Alexandria, came to Ephesus. He was an eloquent man, competent in the Scriptures. He had been instructed in the way of the Lord. And being fervent in spirit, he spoke and taught accurately the things concerning Jesus, though he knew only the baptism of John. He began to speak boldly in the synagogue, but when Priscilla and Aquila heard him, they took him aside and explained to him the way of God more accurately. Acts 18:24-26

Priscilla and Aquila had been taught directly by the Apostle Paul. They were all Jews and tent makers. They met in Corinth and ministered together. What wisdom Priscilla and Aquila must have received about living as a Christian. And what an example of sensitive outreach Paul modeled.

Thus, as they listened to Apollos, Priscilla and Aquila must have looked at each other knowing the other's thoughts. "This Apollos is great. But he doesn't have the full picture. What should we do?"

As they whispered to each other after Apollos finished, did they ask each other questions like: Does God want us to approach Apollos? If so, what does God want us to say?

Those two questions are the foundation of seeking the Lord's guidance as we minister to others.

- What needs to be done?

- Does God want me to do it?

This couple were both sensitive to wanting the full truth of the gospel shared and yet they were also sensitive to Apollos' heart. Notice how they ministered with sensitivity.

- They credited his skills and passion. They didn't throw out everything he said because it was incomplete.

- They recognized the real problem. The challenge was not he didn't have truth. The challenge was he didn't know the whole truth. He was limited, something they most likely pointed out to him. They recognized the background to his training, John the Baptist. When we minister, we need to find out where a person was taught or by whom, in what manner, and what experiences have influenced her belief system. Everything we believe comes from somewhere. We can be sensitive by finding out how a person gained their beliefs.

- Aquila and Priscilla wisely positioned themselves for Apollos' maximum receptivity. I'm sure it must have been hard to not raise their hands to correct him as Apollos was speaking. They must have been concerned the crowd of people would walk away with incomplete knowledge, even misunderstanding. They must have been challenged to trust God to take care of the inadequacy in the minds and hearts of the hearers. Then they approached Apollos and "took him aside." They didn't publicly embarrass him. Now certainly, there might be a time and setting when God leads us to do something publicly, but in this case, it would seem God wasn't leading that way.

- They explained the truth to him "more accurately." They didn't have an all or nothing attitude. "Since you don't know the complete truth, you don't know anything." When you think about it, none of us has the "complete truth." We'll always be learning while on this earth. Thankfully, it would seem Priscilla and Aquila referred to Apollos' level of knowledge building a foundation for Apollos to be more receptive to their correction.

Although we aren't guaranteed of a responsive heart like Apollos, the Acts account tells us he was open to be corrected and "enlarged" in his understanding. As a result, God continued to use him in powerful ways for God's glory as Luke reveals.

And when he wished to cross to Achaia, the brothers encouraged him and wrote to the disciples to welcome him. When he arrived, he greatly helped those who through grace had believed, for he powerfully refuted the Jews in public, showing by the Scriptures that the Christ was Jesus. Acts 18:27-28

I can only imagine the joy and delight Priscilla and Aquila experienced in seeing the fruit of their labors. But I'm also convinced they didn't take credit for the results. They knew God had guided them and he was the source. He deserved the glory.

Reflection and Discussion Questions

1. Do you have a tendency to concentrate more on the mistakes you make to the point you condemn yourself? What are the words you think about yourself?

2. What does your self-contempt say about who God has declared you to be in your position in Christ?

3. How does it feel reading "even mistakes are useable by God for his glory"? Do you agree or disagree?

4. Can you give an example when God used one of your mistakes?

5. Which of Paul's comments to the Corinthians highlighted in this chapter was most meaningful to you? The most difficult to accept or live in?

6. What was your reaction reading about Job's "miserable comforters"?

7. Why do you think Job's friends changed from sensitive to critical?

8. Of the ways Job's friends are "miserable comforters," which do you fall into most often and which do you avoid?

9. Of the suggestions in the section "What Does 'Sensitivity' Look Like?," which one are you weak in and which one are you strong in?

10. Could you use Galatians 2:2, 5 for ministering to someone in any opportunity right now? Remember any kind of interaction with others is ministry.

11. Was there any new insight you found from the comments about Priscilla and Aquila?

Chapter 11
Conclusion
Surprise!

I love surprises, well, at least most of them. When it comes to God's surprises, I admit I don't appreciate them all. But here's a surprise from the Lord I loved.

I first began thinking of this book because I had seen God doing a great work of purification in my own heart's motives. I hope you can tell by now I'm far from having pure motives. But to some degree, I did see a difference. I began wondering if the Lord would want me to share with others. Knowing my books on Christian living books are based on what God has convicted me of and changed in me, it made sense.

As I prayed for wisdom and direction, I began brainstorming about chapter topics. I believed the Lord wanted my writing to be affirming, and I began writing down different benefits—blessings—of giving glory to God from purer motives. And for some reason, many of them started with the letter s. Following the theme, I found more s words that could fit. As non-fiction writers most often do, I formulated what would be included in each chapter of those s words. It all made sense. (Maybe I should have included that s word: sense. Unfortunately, God's work doesn't always make sense, at least in my limited understanding.)

Three-quarters of my way through writing this book, I was thinking of each chapter's "s" words while in my prayer time. As I stared at the list, God seemed to drop an idea into my mind. *I wonder if these correlate to the fruit of the Spirit?* Galatians 5:22-23 gives us that list:

> But the fruit of the Spirit is love, joy, peace, patience, kindness, goodness, faithfulness, gentleness, self-control; against such things there is no law.

I wrote down those nine words in a column and began to look at each of my chapters to see if they related. Although not every characteristic was exact, it seemed to fit. I was excited. God surprised me with his little nudge to see a different aspect of the blessings of being motivated to glorify God: having greater fruit of the Spirit. Here's what I came up with.

Love: *Chapter 2, Selfless: Love Others Well.* This one, of course, corresponds exactly. The chapter focused on the kind of love that gives glory to God through selflessness. I defined love as wanting the best for another person. That's loving "well."

Joy: *Chapter 5, Satisfied: Enjoy Contentment.* Joy and contentment go together. One definition of joy is being satisfied. It's the sense of receiving with joy, fueled by contentment, to rejoice in whatever God designs for us.

Peace: *Chapter 6, Stable: Reap Emotional Strength.* When we're strong in the Lord, we have peace knowing nothing can divert him from empowering us to face life and desire good for us.

Patience: *Chapter 3, Surrendered: Trust God's Plan.* This one isn't quite as directly connected, but when we're surrendered by trusting in God's plan, we patiently wait for him even when the plan is delayed or it is different than expected.

Kindness: *Chapter 8, Struck with Awe: Praise God in Truth.* When we acknowledge God's gracious kindness to us, we pass it along to others.

Goodness: *Chapter 4, Secure: Know Your Position in Christ.* Our ability to react in "good" ways comes from knowing we are secure in our position in Christ. Another aspect is we can never be "good enough" to merit God's love or forgiveness. Our goodness comes from God's gift of salvation through Jesus' sacrificial death.

Faithfulness: *Chapter 9, Steadfast: Exhibit Dependability.* Obviously, this connects exactly. Being steadfast is being faithful.

Gentleness: *Chapter 10, Sensitive: Share God's Design.* The best way to share the gospel with unbelievers and to guide believers to greater wholeness is with a gentle sensitivity to their struggles.

Self-Control: *Chapter 7, Self-Controlled: Choose Rightly.* Amazingly, this is exact.

We all desire to exhibit the fruit of the Spirit. Being more and more pure-hearted will strengthen the Spirit's work in our lives.

If you're still not convinced examining your heart's motives is needed, consider these words from Michael Horton:

Wrapping ourselves in a cocoon of inwardness, we feel cozy in our own personal cult of private piety. We think we're in charge. We imagine that we just follow our heart, that we decide for ourselves what is true, valuable, and useful. In reality, though, our choices are already shaped by the culture of marketing; our preferences have been conditioned by the goods and services, identities and images, possibilities and impossibilities, that have been designed for us in any given moment of this fading age. God's Word comes to release us from this prison that we have mistaken for a palace, as God introduces himself to us and to his world for the first time. God's first word is, "You need to get out more"—out of our cocoon that we have spun for ourselves."[45]

Let's break out of a seemingly comfortable prison—our sinful heart commitments and strategies—and enjoy the freedom of appreciating God's loving motivation for our purity. He wants a heart transformation for our good and his glory, which he deserves. He stands ready to lead the way.

As we close our thoughts about our heart's motives, I'm wondering if you have read this book but aren't sure you have asked and received God's forgiveness resulting in salvation. For many years as a child and teenager, I strived to be "good" and have pure motives. It wasn't until age eighteen I heard the fabulous news of Jesus dying for me to cleanse me of my sins and make me a daughter of the King. What freedom to be relieved of the burden of sin.

Of course, that freedom day, October 1, 1967, was only the beginning of the journey of learning and being purified. It continues to this day. But I can see God's gracious and kind hand upon me continually and faithfully wooing me closer to his loving heart.

If you would like to begin the Christian journey, I invite you to pray something like this—in your own words. "Heavenly Father, I acknowledge I am a sinner. I can never have pure motives in my own efforts. I see now you sent your son Jesus to live on earth, die on the cross for my sins, and rise from the dead to demonstrate victory over death. You have done what I can't do myself. Please forgive me of my sins, both past and future, and strengthen me to live in your power. I know I won't become perfect on this earth, but I look forward with hope to the joy of being glorified in heaven. I pray this in Jesus' Name, Amen."

I would love to hear from you about your prayer or anything else. Please feel free to check out my website: www.KathyCollardMiller. com or email me KathyCollardMiller@gmail.com.

God bless you!

Endnotes

Introduction

1. Owen, John, *The Glory of Christ*, Pavlik Press, 2012, Kindle

2. Moody, Josh and Robin Weekes, *Burning Hearts: Preaching to the Affections*, Christian Focus Publications, 2015, Kindle edition

3. Hamilton, Jr. James M., *God's Glory in Salvation through Judgment: A Biblical Theology*, Crossway, 2010, Kindle edition

Chapter 1

4. VanDrunen, David, *God's Glory Alone*, Zondervan, 2015, page 13

5. Flanagan, Dr. Kelly, "Why Therapists are Clueless", http://drkellyflanagan.com/2015/09/30/why-therapists-are-clueless/, accessed 09/30/2015

Chapter 2

6. Johnson, Jan, "Welcoming the Person in Front of Me", Wisbit e-newsletter, http://janjohnson.org/wisbits_archive.html, accessed August, 2015 (Used by permission.)

7. Tautges, Paul, *Counseling One Another*, Shepherd Press, 2015, Kindle edition

8. Jamieson, Robert, Andrew Robert Fausset, and David Brown, *Commentary Critical and Explanatory on the Whole Bible*, 1871, http://biblehub.com/matthew/6-22.htm, accessed 12/15/15

9. Keller, Timothy, *The Freedom of Self Forgetfulness*, 10Publishing, 2013, Kindle edition

Chapter 3

10. Chandler, Matt, "Youth: Ecclesiastes 11:9-12:8," *The Scriptures Testify about Me: Jesus and the Gospel*, edited by D.A. Carson, Crossway, 2013, Kindle edition

11. McDonald, James, "When You Don't Know What to Do: Psalm 25," *The Scriptures Testify about Me: Jesus and the Gospel*, edited by D.A. Carson, Crossway, 2013, Kindle edition

12. Wilken, Jan, "Choose Hospitality Over Entertaining," http://www.thevillagechurch.net/the-village-blog/choose-hospitality-over-entertaining/, accessed 5/16/16. (Used by permission)

Chapter 4

13. Barrett, Michael P.V. Barrett, Beginning at Moses: *A Guide to Finding Christ in the Old Testament*, Ambassador-Emerald International, 1999, Kindle edition

14. Keller, Timothy, "Getting Out: Exodus 14" in *The Scriptures Testify about Me: Jesus and the Gospel*, edited by D.A. Carson, Crossway, 2013, Kindle edition

15. Lundgaard, Kris, *The Enemy Within: Straight Talk about the Power and Defeat of Sin*, P & R Publishing, 1998, Kindle edition

Chapter 5

16. Nelson, Heather Davis, *Unashamed: Healing Our Brokenness and Finding Freedom from Shame*, Crossway Books, 2016, Kindle edition

17. Tozer, A.W., http://www.therealchurch.com/maxims_and_sayings/tozer.html, accessed 12/08/16

18. Johnson, Jan, http://www.janjohnson.org. Used by permission

19. Jenkins, Bethany, "There's Nothing More Relaxing than Humility", http://www.thegospelcoalition.org/article/theres-nothing-more-relaxing-than-humility?utm_source=The+Gospel+Coalition+Updates&utm_campaign=15835ede15-Best_2015_Update_12_28_2015&utm_medium=email&utm_term=0_a7bb656cd8-15835ede15-290840297, accessed 1/3/16

20. Miller, Kathy Collard, *Why Do I Put So Much Pressure On Myself and Others?*, Xulon Press, 2003, page 13

Chapter 6

21. Michel, Jen Pollock, *Teach Us to Want: Longing, Ambition and the Life of Faith*, IVP Books, 2014, Kindle edition

22. Arthur, Kay, *Lord, I Want to Know You*, WaterBrook Press, 2000, Kindle edition

23. *Teach Us to Want*

24. Thomas, Ian Major Thomas, *The Indwelling Life of Christ: All of Him in All of Me*, Multnomah, 2006, Kindle edition

25. Holcomb, Justin, "God Chooses The Weak And Outcast," http://justinholcomb.com/2012/12/07/god-chooses-the-weak-and-outcast/, accessed 7/9/16

26. Longman III, Tremper, "Getting Brutally Honest with God," *Christianity Today Magazine*, April 2015, page 58

Chapter 7

27. Dean, Jennifer Kennedy, *Altar'd: Experience the Power of Resurrection*, New Hope Publishers, 2012, Kindle edition

28. DeYoung, Rebecca Konyndyk, *Vainglory: The Forgotten Vice*, *Eerdmans*, 2014, Kindle edition

29. Wuest, Kenneth S., *First Peter in the Greek New Testament*, Eerdmans, 1942, page 35

30. *Altar'd*

31. *Altar'd*

32. Nelson, Heather Davis, *Unashamed: Healing Our Brokenness and Finding Freedom From Shame*, Crossway Books, 2016, Kindle edition

33. Smith, Jr., Robert, "Seeing My Son's Murderer: Did I really believe what I preach?" *LeadershipJournal* Winter 2015, Kindle edition

Chapter 8

34. Piper, John, "Must Bible Reading Always End with Application?" transcript and audio, Ask Pastor John, episode 26, desiringGod.org, February 13, 2013, http://www.desiringgod.org/interviews/must-bible-reading-always-end-with-application, accessed 7/20/16

35. Palagy, Pam, *Established: Seeking God's Plan for Spiritual Growth*, Arise Publishing, 2015, Kindle edition

36. Wilund, Jean, "JOY — Illusive, Elusive, or Just Plain Gone?" http://jeanwilund.com/joy-illusive-elusive-or-just-plain-gone-theres-hope-the-joy-of-the-lord-by-rend-collective/, accessed 2/2/16 (Used by permission.)

37. Packer, James, "How I Learned to Live Joyfully," https://thelogcollege.wordpress.com/2015/09/05/how-i-learned-to-live-joyfully-by-james-packer/, accessed 7/29/16

38. Packer, James, *Knowing God*, InterVarsity Press, 1973, page 30

39. Ferguson, Sinclair B., *Let's Study Mark*, Edinburgh: Banner of Truth, 1999, page 116

40. Willard, Dallas, *The Divine Conspiracy*, Harper, 1998, New York, pages 903-4

Chapter 9

41. Lundgaard, Kris, *The Enemy Within*, P&R Publishing, 1998, Kindle edition

42. Brakel, Wilhelmus a', *The Christian's Reasonable Service*, Volume 3, https://biblicalspirituality.files.wordpress.com/2010/03/ reasonableservicevol3-indexed.pdf (accessed 3/9/2017)

Chapter 10

43. Welch, Ed, "Emotions Are A Language," https://www.ccef. org/resources/blog/emotions-are-a-language, August 5, 2016, accessed 1/24/17

44. Foster, Richard, *Freedom of Simplicity: Finding Harmony in a Complex World*, HarperOne, 1973, page 68

Chapter 11

45. Horton, Michael, *The Gospel-Driven Life: Being Good News People in a Bad News World*, Baker Books, 2009, Kindle edition

About the Author

Kathy Collard Miller is best known for her practical Biblical teaching with vulnerable sharing, humor, and motivation woven throughout her speaking and writing. Her ministry began when God delivered her from the sin of abuse of her toddler daughter and restored her broken marriage to Larry.

Her first book telling her story was published in 1984. Since then, Kathy has been in awe of God's plan to develop a ministry with a world-wide impact. She is the best-selling and award-winning author of over fifty books, which feature a full array of nonfiction genres including Bible studies, Bible commentaries, and Christian living topics and has also been an editor of compilation books. Some of her other books are the Daughters of the King Bible study series (*Whispers of My Heart* and *Choices of the Heart*) and *Never Ever Be the Same: A New You Starts Today* (co-written with Larry).

Kathy's articles have appeared in numerous magazines and online sources. She has appeared on hundreds of radio and television programs including The 700 Club.

Kathy is also amazed about the open doors God has given her for speaking. She has spoken in over thirty US states and eight foreign countries including China, Indonesia, and Greece. She loves to see new sights and is so grateful her ministry allows her to travel and see the world.

Kathy and Larry, her husband of almost fifty years, both lay counselors, often write and speak together, especially at marriage events. Kathy and Larry live in Southern California, and are the parents of two and grandparents of two. Contact her at www. KathyCollardMiller.com.